Like a mirage in the desert, the promise of the far country titilates and teases and challenges you to keep going toward it. It promised so much. It delivers, too, but the delivery is transformed into something else in the end. The far country is ghost country. It is a country of shattered dreams, personal disillusionment, diseased bodies, insatiable appetites, lonely crowds, and moral bankruptcy. It ends in a pigpen.

But the prodical can turn homeward. He has a standing invitation. . . . A man can "come to himself" and say, "I will arise and go to my father, and will say unto him, Father, I have sinned against heaven, and before thee." A man can say that, and then start on his way back! —from the book.

THE PLAYBOY COMES HOME

C. M. WARD

Gospel Publishing House
Springfield, Missouri

02-0572

Library of Congress Catalog Card Number 75-32603
International Standard Book Number 0-88243-572-8
Printed in the United States of America

Contents

Foreword

More than any other portion of Scripture the parable of the Prodigal Son has captured C. M. Ward's imagination. During 22 years as *Revivaltime's* speaker, this renowned evangelist has used the Prodigal as his theme 27 times. And people love to hear the way this master of the pulpit portrays the characters of this classic tale that Jesus told.

C. M. Ward has been called the master of the anachronism. That is, he is able to take a Biblical character, dress him up in modern apparel, and place him in today's society. Thus, the Prodigal Son of the first century is transformed by the preacher into the playboy of the 20th century.

Sometimes it is as though C. M. Ward is holding a full-length mirror in which his audience sees themselves in startling clarity. What a wonderful discovery when a crushed and dissipated life awakens to the realization that God is ready to forgive and restore today's playboys and playgirls!

In the pages of this book you will not be visiting the dusty paths of ancient Israel. Instead you will be prowling the streets and alleys of modern America with a perceptive guide at your elbow. He'll point out sights and sounds you might otherwise miss. And he will offer a logical explanation of what you see and hear. Most important of all, he will point to a bright ray of hope. That ray emanates from the preacher's close friend, the Lord Jesus Christ.

I have worked as an editor with C. M. Ward's materials for 10 years. His constant flow of creative genius never ceases to amaze me. I agree with those who have called him the world's greatest radio preacher.

Not only is C. M. Ward a great preacher, he is an outstanding Christian. His travels take him some 200,000 miles every year. Wherever he goes, he treats people with Christian courtesy. He becomes personally acquainted with taxi drivers, waitresses, shoeshine boys, and bellhops. That's because he loves people in all walks of life. He wants to share their triumphs and express his concern for their tragedies.

When one of my children was seriously injured in an automobile accident, this man demonstrated his concern in much more than mere words. He placed a personal check in my hand and assured me that he was willing to do anything he could to assist my family.

C. M. Ward's ministry spans the whole spectrum of Christian service: from pastor to college president, from the pulpits of neighborhood churches to a radio microphone that reaches millions. So I'm sure a delightful time awaits you within the pages of this volume.

E. S. CALDWELL
Pastor, Glad Tidings Assembly of God
Springfield, Missouri

The Parable of the Prodigal

A certain man had two sons: and the younger of them said to his father, Father, give me the portion of goods that falleth to me. And he divided unto them his living. And not many days after the younger son gathered all together, and took his journey into a far country, and there wasted his substance with riotous living. And when he had spent all, there arose a mighty famine in that land; and he began to be in want. And he went and joined himself to a citizen of that country; and he sent him into his fields to feed swine. And he would fain have filled his belly with the husks that the swine did eat: and no man gave unto him. And when he came to himself, he said, How many hired servants of my father's have bread enough and to spare, and I perish with hunger! I will arise and go to my father, and will say unto him, Father, I have sinned against heaven, and before thee, and am no more worthy to be called thy son: make me as one of thy hired servants. And he arose, and came to his father. But when he was yet a great way off, his father saw him, and had compassion, and ran, and fell on his neck, and kissed him. And the son said unto him, Father, I have sinned against heaven, and in thy sight, and am no more worthy to be called thy

9

son. But the father said to his servants, Bring forth the best robe, and put it on him; and put a ring on his hand, and shoes on his feet: and bring hither the fatted calf, and kill it; and let us eat, and be merry: for this my son was dead, and is alive again; he was lost, and is found. And they began to be merry.

Now his elder son was in the field: and as he came and drew nigh to the house, he heard music and dancing. And he called one of the servants, and asked what these things meant. And he said unto him, Thy brother is come; and thy father hath killed the fatted calf, because he hath received him safe and sound. And he was angry, and would not go in: therefore came his father out, and entreated him. And he answering said to his father, Lo, these many years do I serve thee, neither transgressed I at any time thy commandment; and yet thou never gavest me a kid, that I might make merry with my friends: but as soon as this thy son was come, which hath devoured thy living with harlots, thou hast killed for him the fatted calf. And he said unto him, Son, thou art ever with me, and all that I have is thine. It was meet that we should make merry, and be glad: for this thy brother was dead, and is alive again; and was lost, and is found.

Luke 15:11-32

1
Your Right to Choose

The whole plot of the universe is contained in a simple story Jesus told. We call it "The Prodigal Son," and you'll find it in Luke 15:11-32.

Here in this capsule tale is the story of every person—of our right of free choice and what those choices can do to us and to other people.

Every one of us has the chance to prove for himself whether it is really better in "Father's house" or better in the "far country" of our self-will. In that exercise of free will lies all the potential of heartbreak, all the tragedy, all the conquest, all the glory, and all the story of the universe.

THE INALIENABLE RIGHT

No one can deny us our right of choice in the matters that affect our ultimate happiness or misery. The younger son in this family story demanded the right early in life. "Give me the portion of goods that falleth to me," he challenged (v. 12).

He couldn't wait to cut loose from family restraints. He couldn't stay home long enough to inherit his portion. He didn't want to work for it. He wasn't prepared to earn it.

"Give me. . . . " Human nature has changed little since that time.

This young man may have been brilliant, but he had no sense of accountability, because he had not come to grips with the three basic questions of life: Where did I come from? Why am I here? Where am I going?

He just wanted to get away from restraint, away from responsibility, from accountability. He didn't know where he was going, but he was in a hurry to get there. The world offered so much to see. It offered all kinds of things to do. Life was there for the taking, for the touching, for the tasting, for the handling.

His pockets burned for money he had not earned. His heart burned for the chance to enjoy the pleasures of the world for a season. How soon he would learn that besides all these, there was so much to be.

This universal story has been repeated many times on many stages, with many actors. Long before Jesus talked about this impulsive young man, the Bible says Esau had this same spirit. "What profit shall this birthright do to me?" he asked in a moment of fleshly appetite. He determined to set his own course. The immediate demands of his tastebuds and his stomach were more important to him than his soul, his mind, or his conscience—not to mention his future.

"Esau was a cunning hunter, a man of the field . . . and Esau said to Jacob, Feed me . . . with that same red pottage." Never mind the price. "Give me. . . . "

The reckoning could wait. His appetite couldn't. Or so he reasoned. But Esau lost more than he ever regained in the choice he based on expediency.

I'll guarantee you one thing, when you walk the self-will road without regard for God or man, you'll be in want before you get all the way to the end of that road.

It won't take you long to go through the soup or the substance. The road that leads away from the Father's house promises you that. Something will gnaw on you worse than the hogs—it's the *waste*.

You start with a good pair of eyes. They are piercing, clear, have perfect color and focus. They never know a moment of pain or blurring. Take inventory! Somewhere along the road of self-will they grow red and lusterless. Your eyelids droop. The nerves in your face twitch. The eyes no longer track correctly.

You start with a first-rate heart. You can race. You can lift. You can swim for distance. There isn't a hitch. There isn't a murmur. It gets different along the way somewhere. Riotous living will send you a bill to be paid. You have the agony and mental strain of knowing you could drop at any moment. You have to make excuses for yourself. The motor is no longer reliable. *Waste!*

On this road you'll feel hell long before you get there. Hell is the eternity of waste.

The hard road back home is not an easy one. A lot of people never make it because they can't get past the "Give me" stage to the "Make me" stage which comes later in this story. But keep your heart open. People do make the long journey back. They make it every day. God's mercy makes it possible.

THE UNUTTERABLE ANGUISH

There is more than one character on the stage when the playboy takes off for the far country. No man lives to himself. His parents share the stage with him, and a lot of interested friends are there too. Granted, some parents could care less when the young person takes his portion and goes out the door. But a lot more of them care than some young people would like to believe.

Through the tender years they hope, they train. They educate. They pray and counsel; they shelter and nurture. But no parent, no friend, can force a decision.

Always the parents live with the knowledge in their hearts that the day will come when their offspring will "gather all together, and take his journey."

Parents cannot postpone that moment indefinitely. They recognize the inalienable right of their children to make their own biggest choices. The right of choice is God-given and God-protected.

With what unutterable rejoicing parents watch as their children make the basic choices that lead to a successful career and a God-honoring life.

And with what unspeakable anguish countless parents have watched their sons and daughters "gather all together" and start for a far country that can only lead to heartache for all concerned.

You may never see their tears, or hear them cry aloud. But I have read their letters by the hundred in the course of my radio ministry. How often they echo the anguished cry of David for his rebellious son. Weeping as he went, David mourned, "O my son Absalom! my son, my son Absalom! would God I had died for thee, O Absalom, my son, my son!" (2 Samuel 18:33).

BEYOND YOUR POWER

A young woman asked for police intervention because of her fear of a certain person who had threatened to kill her. Law enforcement officers insisted they were not in a position to do anything even though she was convinced a crime was likely to take place. They explained they were an apprehending agency whose duty it was to catch the offender after the crime was committed. They knew they could not make people do right. As long as there is a "far country" there will be those who insist on making the trip.

The answer, to the person who is determined to take the road to the far country, is not in power, even though absolute authority be used for another's good.

This principle is as true of nations as it is of individuals. Our own nation, powerful though it seems, is finding that you cannot coerce another nation to go a certain way if that nation does not choose to do so. From our point of view, democracy may be the best form of government, but we cannot compel another to accept it on that basis. We think we know how other countries could raise their standards of living and be at peace with one another at the same time. But we cannot, even with all our apparent power and goodwill, force our way of living and our standards and values upon another people.

The right of choice for nations is as ultimately theirs as it is for individuals. We do not have it in our power to make even the best of choices for them.

Human nature being what it is, there is another important consideration. Even if we were able to force our will upon others, and even though we might look upon ourselves as benevolent dictators in doing so, there would still be a fly in that ointment. The people for whom we would try to choose would hold a deep smoldering resentment for us because we took away their right—their inalienable right—to make their own choice.

No, there is no way for us to arbitrarily prevent another from going the way of waste, riotous living, and bankruptcy, both spiritually and literally. We can plead, we can suggest, we can pray, but the choice is ultimately theirs. Not even God takes away the prerogative of choice. He asks, He pleads, He calls, He even came in the person of His Son. But the choice stays in our hands. It is the divine plan.

The sob of the Master is repeated, with some variation, in many of today's headlines: "O Jerusalem, Jerusalem, thou that killest the prophets, and stonest them which are sent unto thee, how often would I have gathered thy children together, even as a hen gathereth her chickens under her wings, and *ye would not!* Behold, your house is left unto you desolate" (Matthew 23:37, 38).

THE BETTER WAY

I've tried to make it quite clear already that I am aware that one human being can't force another human being to choose the right way. That inalienable right of choice is something I believe in and practice.

In the capsule account of the Prodigal Son that Jesus gave us, He didn't take time to insert what remarks if any the father may have made when his son began to get itchy feet and start "getting it all together" for the big adventure. He didn't take time to tell us what the father thought when his son boldly asked for what was coming to him from the father's goods. What did the father think as he gave his son "the portion of goods that falleth to me"?

I won't speculate, but that won't keep me from making a few observations of my own, and here they are.

Food is better than famine. Love is better than loneliness. Merriment is better than misery. Forgiveness is better than being a fugitive. Responsibility is better than renunciation. Compassion is better than condemnation. A robe is better than rags. Life is better than death. And to be found is better than to be lost and wandering far from the Father's house. The difference between having one or the other is in the choices we make.

It's always a tragedy to learn we've made a wrong choice. The tuition in the school of self-will is expensive. It was for this young man Jesus told about. For him it led to bankruptcy, famine, loneliness, shabbiness, guilt. But eventually—thank God—it led him home, because he faced the problem squarely and did something about it.

The "Give me" attitude pervades our society today. Too many think only in terms of what they can get. They figure God owes them health, adventure, profit, a chance to investigate evil without paying the bill. All these they intend to use without measure, and charge it to a jovial, generous God as experience.

But there comes a sobering moment when a look down the road tells you something. It tells you that it is not what you can get from the Father through conniving and rebellion that counts, but rather it is what the Father can do for you and through you by His grace and love.

YOU CAN BLOW YOUR LIFE—OR LIVE IT

Your Heavenly Father will guide your life if you will let Him. But He'll never in time or eternity violate your right of choice. "He was not willing that any should perish," the Bible says, and then that sentence ends with what we can do about it. The whole sentence reads, "The Lord is . . . not willing that any should perish, but that all should come to repentance" (2 Peter 3:9).

17

Look around you today and you'll see a lot of people who have come to God through repentance and found the better way to live. Even secular magazines carry the testimonies of men and women who took the wrong road one time, and ended up where they never expected to be in terms of sin and heartache. When they realized the way to get back, they turned their lives over to the only One who could help them—and this was still free choice—and He made them new creatures in Christ Jesus.

God made Billy Sunday an evangelist seen and heard by millions. He made George Washington and his ragged unpaid troops changers of history. He made J.C. Penney, an obscure storekeeper who trusted Him, a multimillionaire. He made Martin Luther a reformer who changed the history of the world.

Get beyond the "give-me" stage, and talk to God about what He might want to do in you and through you. You won't have to talk long. A prayer like that stirs another world. And the happiness you'll feel in the center of God's will for your life beats anything you could ever experience in a life of riotous living.

Listen to Paul's testimony. Here's a man who once walked down the wrong road, but when he got a chance to make a different choice, he made it—fast. Now he could say, "But what things were gain to me, those I counted loss for Christ" (Philippians 3:7). When you let Jesus into your situation, your sense of priorities changes for the better. You are in the hands of somebody bigger than you are, and better too! You're teamed up with a winner, so you can't keep on being a loser.

Now listen to John's testimony! This man was once an ordinary fisherman who was more interested in the next catch of fish than anything else in life. Then he looked up and saw Jesus coming down the road and that made all the difference. Everybody is somebody in the kingdom of God. John said of Jesus that He "hath made us kings and priests unto God" (Revelation 1:6).

I once spent an afternoon with Walter Knott, Sr., developer of the famous Knott's Berry Farm operation in Southern California. His philosophy, as he explained it to me, was that God expects each of us to leave this planet an even more attractive place than it was when we arrived. He worked hard and sacrificially at such a task—taking acres that were practically desert and sage, and in a life span he created park and pleasure, a source of enjoyment and education for millions.

Mr. Knott acknowledged an obligation toward his Creator. He engaged in a service. And God is never in anyone's debt. The Knott corporation today is worth millions.

I'll tell you this. You'll get better treatment as a servant of God than you'll ever experience as a rebel. God can pay His friends better than Satan can his slaves.

God can take total failure, a stumblebum —shredded, filthy, degraded, company for swine —and make that person a new person. God does it. It is His prerogative and He takes the initiative when you turn to Him. When you choose, He's waiting. "But as many as received him, to them gave he power to become the sons of God" (John 1:12).

Don't blow your life! Live it to the full as God intended it to be. Paul saw what happened to him, what led him astray. He said he was "blinded" by the god of this world. He was misled. He was seduced. He had thought life meant getting, spending on self,

19

going for broke. All of that changed when he met Jesus on the Damascus road. He chose Jesus as Lord, and asked the big question, "Lord, what wilt thou have me to do?" (Acts 9:6).

That playboy Jesus told about in Luke 15 lived to understand that the pride of life could consume a person in his passion to get. It left Germany in a shambles because of Hitler. It left Napoleon in exile. It left Egypt humiliated and Pharaoh dead.

Let's confess it. You and I don't know how to use God's gifts without God's guidance. Choice is our right, but for both the high and the mighty and the poor and the downtrodden, wrong choices start us on wrong roads. We need God's grace and God's guidance to show us how to live beyond the "Give me" stage.

2
A Bad Trip

Choice leads to action. It did for the Prodigal Son. It will for you. That's the course of things. You read the ads about that far country out there where there's no parental restraint, no church to say where it's leading you, no voices calling you back, and you begin to have that insatiable desire to check it out for yourself.

The call of the far country starts you on a bad trip. Eve found it out in the Garden of Eden. And every generation insists on proving it all over again.

In Jesus' thumbnail sketch of human nature, He portrays the father as yielding to his son's choice:

"And he divided unto them his living. And not many days after the younger son gathered all together, and took his journey into a far country . . . " (Luke 15:12, 13).

This was actually the last time the young man ever "got it all together." From then on, he was scattering his inheritance just as fast as he could. And he learned the hard way that it is easier to throw away your heritage than it is to get it back.

Thousands of young people have prided themselves on "going on a trip" propelled by some combination of chemicals forced into their bloodstreams. This is how they started into the far country, some of them never to return. It takes a miracle to get back!

THE SEAMY SIDE

A well-known go-go dancer, thirteen years in the business, granted a candid interview to a staff member of a big city newspaper. In the course of the interview she opened up her life and let the reporter see what it was really like—the sleaziness, the frustration, the indignities she suffered in that far country.

"I was told all my life by my old-fashioned Christian parents that I shouldn't do it," she said. "But I thought dancing would bring me glamor and exciting night life."

But it didn't, she admitted. What it did bring her, among other humiliating and painful experiences, were heartaches, two broken marriages, serious family problems, insecurity, a worn-out body and an unstable future.

Offering her body for public use by implication brought her incredible propositions by both male and female customers. She had witnessed and participated in acts not fit to mention even in a newspaper, let alone in this book. She tolerated the insults and humiliation because her 11 a.m. to 9 p.m., six-days-a week exposure of her aging flesh was a way of making a living in that far country. At home she had a child to support.

During those 13 years she had been shot, knifed, slugged, and beaten, as well as applauded. "If you had it to do over again, would you choose this profession?" the reporter asked.

"If I had it to live over? NO. I would not do it again," she said emphatically. "I have been hardened to the point where sex makes me sick. I'll never marry again because of my experiences in these past 13 years."

What does her child think? "My daughter asks me, 'Mommy, why do you work at a bar?' I try to explain. She'll say, 'Mommy, I still love you,' and it hurts. There are better ways of making a living than getting beer thrown in your face, having your body pawed by drunks, and hearing slurs. . . . " Then she sighed to the reporter, "My Christian parents keep on waiting."

The lure of a trip to the far country draws all too many unsuspecting persons with an irresistible attraction. It's a whirl, and it's wild. It promises endless partying and carefree living. You are away out there somewhere, without guidelines and free from the inhibitions that seem to have held you back. The lust of the flesh catapults you into dangerous situations. The lure of the far country is very real. Satan meant it to be that way.

Yet I do not think anyone who starts ever intends to get so far away. One of our nation's celebrities experienced a tragedy in his own family when his daughter took her bad trip into a far country. Her grieving father could only conclude that "Over the months she found she had a tiger in her bloodstream."

LIKE A MIRAGE

Like a mirage in the desert, the promise of the far country titilates and teases and challenges you to keep going toward it. It promises so much. It delivers, too, but the delivery is transformed into something else in the end.

The far country is ghost country. It is a country of shattered dreams, personal disillusionment, diseased bodies, insatiable appetites, lonely crowds, and moral bankruptcy. It ends in a pigpen.

You are tormented for the very things you have

23

thrown away, and you are sick of what you paid everything to get. You remember with anguish the love and respect of those who trusted you. You hate the rags and the filth. You are appalled at the losses that accumulate.

In his exceptional documentary—*The Red Orchestra*—the anatomy of the most successful spy ring of World War II, Gilles Perrault sketched in detail the last moments and final thought of some of the agents caught and executed by German Counterintelligence.

One of these agents penned his last words from the far country before his execution:

Dear Parents,
So the time has come; another few hours and I shall be parting company with myself. . . . You two are now suffering both a loss and a feeling of shame, and this you have not deserved. Time will soften your sorrow. . . . I shall be thinking until the very end of the last look my father gave me. I shall be thinking of my darling Mama's tears. It has taken these last months to bring me so close to you—I, your prodigal son. . . . After so much impulsiveness and passion, after following so many paths which seemed so strange to you, I have finally found my way home. . . . Yes, and now I reach out my hand to you all. . . . "

NAKED TRUTH

The far country is filled with hallucinations. After Art Linkletter's daughter took her fatal bad trip, he probed more deeply into the nature of that far country in the hope of helping others who fell into the same trap. He found out some things.

"Those kids I've talked to who use it [drugs] tell me that when you're on what they call a downer, with a heavy dose of LSD, every one of your faults and shortcomings stands in stark, naked, unrelieved, unrationalized relief. There is no place to hide."

The naked truth is more than many can bear to face about themselves.

24

Judas reached that far country, and he found indifference instead of sympathy, phantoms instead of friends, just when he faced the naked truth about himself.

So he was a traitor. So he had sinned. So he had betrayed innocent blood. So he had 30 pieces of silver he couldn't bear to keep or spend. "What is that to us?" those who had beckoned him into that far country asked. "See thou to that" (Matthew 27:4).

As the onetime friends fall back one by one, your conscience cries the louder. It did in Judas. Memories of better days stir within. They did in Judas. A wave of shame engulfs your soul. It did in Judas. The sweet promise of the far country turns to gall which has no equal for bitterness. It did for Judas.

ASHES

The lure of the far country has been around for a long time. It can strike in the best of families, in the most affluent circumstances, and on the highest-rated campuses. It leaves a toll of waste—decayed and almost forgotten civilizations, unmarked and unacknowledged graves; vandalism; shattered economies; shredded marriages; innocent victims who accidentally got in the way; and *ashes* when it has finally burned itself out.

Jezebel in her time went to the far country. She married a fellow named Ahab and took him with her. She decided to run God out of the country. She hated preachers. Neither drought nor famine abated her hatred.

Those of God's people she could not murder, she drove to caves. She directed taxpayers to palaces of iniquity. She filled the country with discotheques. Swingers took their cue from "prophets of the groves . . . which did eat at Jezebel's table" (1 Kings 18:19).

Jezebel vowed to tear in pieces the contract God had written with Israel. In keeping with her plan, she sent this message to the evangelist who dared to challenge her: "So let the gods do to me, and more also, if I make not thy life as the life of one of them by tomorrow about this time" (1 Kings 19:2).

In the far country of her rebellion, Jezebel smeared the reputations of good men and considered it not robbery to confiscate their possessions to please her husband. She told him, "Arise, and eat bread, and let thine heart be merry: I will give thee the vineyard of Naboth" (1 Kings 21:7).

Lies, murder, treason, blackmail, demonstration, temper tantrums, intimidation, sex, and violence —these were her everyday tools. The nation cowered at her feet. She wrote a saga of recklessness. It is all there in your Bible. Centuries later, the name of Jezebel still conjures up memories of what the far country of self-will and rebellion is like.

How did Jezebel's trip to the far country end? How did this fusillade against law and order, against decency and morals, against respect for property and life finally end? Here's the record:

"Jezebel . . . looked out a window. . . . And [Jehu] said, Throw her down. So they threw her down: and some of her blood was sprinkled on the wall, and on the horses: and he trode her under foot.

"And when he was come in, he did eat and drink, and said, Go, see now this cursed woman, and bury her: for she is a king's daughter. And they went to bury her: but they found no more of her than the skull, and the feet, and the palms of her hands.

"Wherefore they came again, and told him. And he

said, This is the word of the Lord, which he spake by his servant Elijah the Tishbite, saying, In the portion of Jezreel shall dogs eat the flesh of Jezebel: and the carcass of Jezebel shall be as dung on the face of the field . . . " (2 Kings 9:30-37).

However Jezebel had envisioned her last trip, she certainly never imagined it would be an involuntary trip down from an upstairs window to savage dogs in the courtyard below. None of us envision the kind of ignominious end that we see people in the far country coming to every day. Our news media keep us informed and spare none of the graphic details. But it's always somebody else. We think we can circumvent that course of events for ourselves. But if you follow that far country road to the end of the line, you'll find what everyone else has found: the bad trip has a bad ending.

SIN IS INSANITY

This glimpse of the far country comes from the broken heart of a disappointed wife:

My husband was a handsome, intelligent young man. He came from a good religious family. Our marriage was thought to be one of the perfect matches of all time. Then he discovered marijuana. At first it was a kick. . . . Soon it was more—benzedrine, then dexedrin, then methedrine. He was taking pills to sleep, pills to wake up, pills to keep going during the day. . . .

Then I expected a child. . . . My husband would not, or could not, quit. Since I was unwilling to turn on with him, he found friends who would. Our apartment soon became a gathering place for potheads, pillheads, acid users, cocaine sniffers, and other assorted drug abusers. . . . I saw my husband become a stranger to me. . . . He could not stand the thought of having a straight wife. . . . Then he started to abuse our infant son. He didn't want my help. . . . Some day I want my son to be proud of his mother, and I want him to understand that his father would love him if he could. . . . But he's sick.

Now, that's a far country! That's the trip away from restraint your friends promise you. Yes, there are

27

"pushers"—merchants of hell always ready to give you a gentle shove down the road for a modest investment. They may even finance your first mile, but they'll forsake you long before you walk that last disastrous mile. A trip into that far country will totally bankrupt you before you arrive in that never-never land.

Hell won't settle for any less. It will bleed you white. It will scuttle you. It will strip you of everything decent and worthwhile. That was what Satan was after when he enticed Eve. That's what he's after in your situation. "Spend all!" he says. "Have a blast!" He never lets you hold anything in reserve.

ANYBODY CAN GO

Lest you get the idea that only the Jezebels and the worst kind of people can ever land in a far country, let me tell you about a proud, successful evangelist who went there.

His name was Jonah, and he made a wrong turn at what might have been a high point in his career. At the very least, his bad trip was a humiliating and painful journey that brought experiences he need never have known. Even though he ended up doing what God wanted him to in the first place, the whole episode is remembered because of his bad trip.

Jonah never intended to head toward the far country. "But Jonah rose up to flee unto Tarshish from the presence of the Lord." There are always those who wait to offer you passage when you want to get to a far country. "He found a ship . . . so he paid the fare thereof." That is, he *thought* he did. He found out what many others have discovered—that money doesn't always pay all the fare. He was to learn by bitter experience the full cost of disobedience.

28

"And there was a mighty tempest." The sunny weather soon changes to storms on the trip a world system promises you. Sin will dump you when you least expect it. The pleasure ride ends abruptly when you are fleeing "from the presence of the Lord." "So they took up Jonah, and cast him forth into the sea."

If you survive at all, you head into rough company! There isn't much sentiment when you are heading the wrong way—when you're a loser. The fast set will cut you. The bouncer shows you the door. Your credit's no good. You're not good company any more. You're washed up!

Here is Jonah's testimony! "The waters compassed me about, even to the soul: the depth closed me round about, the weeds were wrapped about my head. I went down to the bottoms. . . ." "Out of the belly of hell cried I" (Jonah 2:5, 6, 2).

Yet Jonah came back. It's a different journey back. It starts when you have had enough. For Jonah it began when he cried out of the belly of that whale, and God cared enough to hear that cry in high heaven. That kind of cry is what God is waiting for.

But crying is not enough. Judas wept, but his tears fell short of repentance. Jonah went all the way and God heard him. That's the difference.

IT'S BETTER NOT TO GO

If there's forgiveness and restoration for those who take that trip to the far country, then why not go and have your fling, then holler for help when the going gets rough enough? That's a question every generation grapples with. It sounds plausible enough. I'll have my cake and eat it too, they think. But if ever you are tempted with this thought, look around you at some who have made it back to Father's house.

The grace of God is given to bring you back home, but there are scars and entanglements that are not changed overnight, and some not forever. What do you do, for example, with the knowledge that you have become the parent of a child who suffers because of your bad trip? How do you handle the marital disasters of which you have been a part? Can you give back the life and virtue of the innocent who followed in his footsteps to that far country? Each trip brings its own private, personal tragedies and heartaches that only God can help you live with and turn into triumphs of His grace.

Ask the man who's been there. Ask the woman who made the trip. They'll tell you that even if by God's matchless grace they made it back, they wish they'd never gone. There's so much to forget. So much time and strength misspent, never to be regained.

It's better not to go.

3
Flat Broke

A bad trip with full pockets is one thing. It's another blow to turn those pockets inside out one day and find them empty. But that's the way it goes.

In Jesus' unfolding portrait of the universal prodigal, He lists the next step: ". . . and there wasted his substance with riotous living. And when he had spent all, there arose a mighty famine in that land; and he began to be in want" (Luke 15:13, 14).

NO CREDIT

It's an ugly moment when you are turned down by everyone. "And no man gave unto him" (Luke 15:16). The briefly wealthy young man had become known as a bad risk. His credit had run out.

A "credibility gap" is neither pleasant nor valuable. You haven't achieved anything desirable when no one will believe you any more. You have established an unenviable record when you have sold the only body you will ever have in this life for whatever it would bring.

It may amuse some when the subject for entertainment for stage or screen is the drunkard who sprawls in some doorway with only a container of canned heat for company. But it doesn't do much for the thinking man. It doesn't amuse the man they mimic. That kind of thing is too close to the painful truth of his dreadful and abject poverty of body, mind, and spirit—not to mention the flatness of his wallet.

Your credit has run out. You have nowhere to go except to the pigpen, and out. If bankruptcy is your target—consciously or not—you can reach it in a hurry in the far country. You can easily and quickly "waste your substance." That's not difficult. Spending money and more than money can become a way of life. By it you'll reach the reality of the far country sooner than you expect. The jolt will be insolvency.

The first time a bartender says to you, "I'm sorry, I can't let you have it on the cuff this time," you'll get a jolt. When you realize he isn't going to extend any further credit, and the source of your thirst-quencher is cut off—you'll feel the first real impact of what sin does to a fellow.

The first time the clerk looks at you through the dimly-lighted smoke-filled air of a rooming house that's one step above a flophouse and says profession-ally, "I'm sorry. We don't have a room available. You might try elsewhere," you will begin to understand the "want" of a far country. You'll experience a thud—a letdown. You will grope in unreality. You will ask a thousand times before daybreak, "Where has it all gone? What did I do with it?"

It can be life's darkest moment when you begin to be in want. When you know what it means to be flat broke, literally, morally, spiritually, and "no man gives to you"—no man.

Your fingers aren't walking through the Yellow Pages then, a preferred customer making the choice of where his valued business will go. No, you're a has-been—a human tragedy, riffraff to the world—but not to God. You are through, as far as the world is concerned—without market value. You won't find it exciting. You'll discover it's a nightmare.

CHEATED

Oh, the panic of bad checks that bounce, of notices stamped on your intentions, which read "insufficient funds"! Oh, the terrible sense of the fugitive, when you cringe at every knock on the door, dreading the bill collector! Oh, the utter shame when you read the notice of eviction! Oh, the humiliation of seeing your automobile or furniture repossessed!

"When he had spent all"—and there's nothing left to meet the pressing needs that go on for yourself and your family.

You remember when you once perfunctorily pulled out identification for the clerk to see when you wanted to write a check for groceries. You drummed your fingers nonchalantly on the counter in those days of plenty, not minding that she checked the list of bad risks. You weren't a bad risk, but condescendingly you understood and tolerated the clerk's lack of knowledge of your comfortable bank balance. Now that same minor annoyance turns into frozen terror when your name gets on that bad risk list. It's a moment so close to hell that you think you might as well be there.

Who can have pride in that moment? You crawl. You turn from the gambling table. Your last chip has been raked in. Every asset is liquidated. The crowd turns away. Dame Chance has scorned you. She has many suitors, many lovers. She is unfaithful to all. She is a lady of caprice. Her smile is wanton. Her promises are vague. Her favorites come and go. She bleeds you white. She discards you as pulp, rind, skin. You feel *cheated,* taken, beaten, a fool.

I promise you, it will take more than a shrug of a shoulder in that moment, an attitude of "who cares"—of "easy-come-easy-go." You may manage a halfhearted laugh on the outside, but you'll be bleeding on the inside, for it's a stark moment when the world tells you firmly your credit is no good.

You'll feel hollow and rejected when there's nothing left. You are wrinkled and blotched and scabbed until the magic of cosmetics can no longer hide your overdrawn account. You didn't think it would end this way at all when you gathered all together and began your journey to the far country. You had so much going for you, you reasoned. But now it's all faded and frayed.

If you're not there yet, go down to skid row and take a look at those who made the trip all the way. That wild, wild thing you have going for you is priced high. It will take everything you have.

FALSE AND EMPTY

It doesn't take some people long to know they are on the wrong road, and that the road won't bring them what they expected from the trip. What is tragic is that they don't know or can't bring themselves to take the way back. A young man in Louisiana became convinced he was not making the kind of life he started out to get in the far country. Too young to be that far from home, and too proud to go back, he wrote a poignant farewell note and hanged himself from a persimmon tree.

In a story reported by the Associated Press, he is quoted as writing in the note, "When you stop growing you are dead. I stopped growing long ago. I never

34

did develop into a real person and I can't tolerate the false and empty existence I have created."

How badly he was in want—spiritually, emotionally, and God only knows in how many other ways —is shown in his pathetic evaluation of his frustrations:

"What frustrated me most in the last year was that I had built no ties to family or friends. There was nothing of lasting worth and value. I led a detached existence and I was a parody of a person—literally and figuratively. I didn't tell jokes—I *was* a joke."

In a final note to his parents on a separate scrap of paper, he acknowledged, "You have provided me excellent advantages and privileges and experiences. I am extremely grateful for all of your sacrifices, time, and support. . . . "

The story gives no hint that the young man saw his problem as a spiritual one, and this is not the place for conjecture. Still, that searching spirit, that emptiness of mind and soul and body that cries out so painfully for satisfaction, finds no lasting fulfillment in anything the far country has to offer.

Augustine knew this terrible craving emptiness and when he groped back from the far country, he exclaimed, "Thou hast made us for thyself, and we never rest till we rest in Thee." The divine spark in everyone of us waits for the breathing of the Spirit of God upon it to fan it into a flame of life that makes us a whole person.

WASTE BRINGS WANT

The Prodigal Son "wasted his substance in riotous living . . . and he began to be in want."

There comes a moment when you realize how unfulfilled you are—how terribly dissatisfied you are

35

with the person you have become. It happened to this lad. He got there. He strewed his father's goods along a spendthrift path. He embarked on a career of waste and disregard that led straight to famine and bankruptcy. He got there as fast as he could.

His course started with the "give-me's"—the idea that you can make a go of it without work. "Give me the goods!" He had the idea that it was his right to spend what someone else had earned. He was not a worker but a waster. And there are a lot of wasters today. Their text is the same, "Give us the goods!"

Here are some lines by an unknown author that say a great deal to us today:

> There are a lot of men who creep
> Into the world to eat and sleep,
> And know no reason why they're born
> Save only to consume the corn,
> Devour the cattle, bread and fish,
> And leave behind an empty dish;
> And if their tombstones, when they die,
> Were not to flatter or to lie,
> There's nothing better can be said
> Than that they've eaten up their bread,
> Drunk up their drink, and gone to bed.

I will tell you this. You will come to want unless you realize that your trip from the cradle to the coffin is a partnership. You will discover you cannot make it by yourself. There is no possible way to make it without your Father's help. That lesson comes too late for some folk.

There is something more. It is a stubborn fact to face, but your Creator has a job for you to do. It may not be to your liking or wanting, but God has something He needs you to do nevertheless. This planet was not made for freeloaders. This is a work world.

You can rebel. This young man did, and others have. You can take the attitude that the world owes you a living. But you cannot change the result of that attitude. A sense of want will set in. You will eventually be filled with loathing for yourself—for the knowledge that you have accomplished nothing —that you are nothing, and that you have understood nothing. The vexation of it all is the worst nausea possible to experience.

This partnership is a stewardship. Try to grab pieces of it for yourself, and you will lose it all! The earth is the Lord's. You cannot take it with you. It is entrusted to our care. We are custodians, not owners. We are partners with God, not spectators. The soil itself lets us know when we neglect it.

The dust storm will teach you. The roaring flood will teach you. The polluted air will teach you. You have got to put something back when you take something out. There are laws to respect.

Land greed can grind the soil to dust. Recklessly whipping the timber off the land can erode the top soil and wash away the productive layers that nature has so patiently built. Belching out fumes and smoke and grime can take a toll of lives.

We learn the hard way, but we learn. You just cannot ignore God's plan and have it all your own way. Never! Stewardship is real enough. We have to keep giving back in order to keep getting.

Neglect a garden and you reap a wilderness. There have been a lot of "Adams" in history. God wants you for a partner, but if you want it all by yourself the opportunity is yours. It's that matter of choice all over again. But the way of the transgressor is hard.

Waste brings want. Waste is the repudiation of stewardship. Waste is a result of lack of respect. This principle applies whether we're talking about land or bodies or souls or lives. If we waste, we want. If we determine to act responsibly as good stewards of what God has put into our power, we find ourselves in partnership with the God of the universe. You can't lose when He's your partner. You can't win when He's not.

ON ANOTHER'S CREDIT

I've often heard quartets sing, "Where could I go but to the Lord.... Needing a friend, to help me in the end.... Seeking a refuge for my soul...." That's a plaintive plea based on the big problem: Where can I find credit when I have none?

Jesus told a story about such a debtor. "But forasmuch as he had not to pay, his lord commanded him to be sold, and his wife, and children, and all that he had, and payment to be made. The servant therefore fell down, and worshipped him, saying, Lord, have patience with me, and I will pay thee all. Then the lord of that servant was moved with compassion, and loosed him, and forgave him the debt" (Matthew 18:25-27). Jesus gave that account to reflect the heart of God toward the debtor, the sinner.

Others will foreclose without mercy. There's no sentiment. A debt is to be collected, if not in one way, then in another.

What you need is someone to cancel those debts. You need more than patience on the part of your creditors when you're broke. God has waited for you already through years of broken IOU's. You have involved your wife and your children. They are bonded by your huge debt of drinking and profanity and reckless living and temper. You're all at the brink. Now what will you plead—more patience? Your worthless promise to square every bill you owe?

I'll tell you this: If God couldn't find love in His

38

eternal heart for you, there would be no hope at all. But the Bible says, "Then the lord of that servant was moved with compassion, and loosed him, and forgave him the debt" (Matthew 18:27).

If He doesn't loose you—break those fetters on your soul and mind, deliver you from the hell that waits —all the forgiveness of heaven won't help you. The compounded trouble you have made for yourself will swamp you. But he "loosed him, and forgave him the debt," and He can do the same for you. Salvation is more than an emotional, tearful scene. It's a sweet deliverance.

That's what Jesus did for the dying thief. That man's credit had run out. He offered no excuse. He reminded the thief on the third cross that they were hanging there "justly; for we receive the due reward of our deeds" (Luke 23:41).

That man would never have made it into paradise had he not traveled on another's credit. There was not an item he could mortgage. There was not a cosigner for him in that gaping crowd. Who would sign for a thief nailed to timber? What assets could he offer as collateral? But God sent Someone to sign for him. "I say unto thee, Today shalt thou be with me in paradise," Jesus said. He signed for that thief because the thief turned to Him without reservation, without hope in himself, but with a trace of faith. "Lord, remember me . . . ," he pleaded. That's the difference between heaven and hell in a life.

Heaven's credit begins when you have "spent all." So long as you think you can make it by yourself, you don't know you need Jesus. You don't know you need grace. You don't know you need heaven. You don't know you need Calvary. Calvary is for sinners. That hill is for the insolvent. That cross beckons the broken and the beaten. It welcomes the crushed and contrite. It offers unlimited capital for just one signature on that line in the application that reads, "I have sinned . . . and am no more worthy" (Luke 15:18).

God will listen to you. He will reach you. That altar you approach—whether it's shaped like a bedside or a tree stump or even a barstool—is an altar of grace, not merit or fashion or ability, when you come in humility.

"By grace are ye saved . . . it is the gift of God" (Ephesians 2:8). God extends toward you all that you need. He offers long-term credit to people the world considers bad risks. It's incredible. No wonder men call it the greatest story ever told.

There's no waiting period, no probation. Help is present. It's right here. I've reached so many times toward these words: "God is our refuge and strength, a very present help in trouble" (Psalm 46:1). When you come to Jesus, you've been turned down for the last time. Others may fail and turn away, but the Son of God will stay by you.

The call is for failures. "He that hath no money; come ye, buy" (Isaiah 55:1). That's the invitation. That's credit. It's the best feeling your soul will ever experience.

Hell will make you crawl. It will whip you. It will bend you and destroy you. It will bounce you out of places where once you paid your way. It will disown the smell it forced upon you. It will refer you to the gutter. You can check the facts by a million testimonies in the heart of New York, Chicago, Philadelphia, and Los Angeles—and even at the corner bar in a thousand smaller towns.

Heaven alone is prepared to extend you credit when you're flat broke. The Father cares that much.

4
You Can't Make It On Husks

Sin will eventually reduce its slaves to the level of swine. Jesus' story of the lost son swiftly outlines the steps from arrogance to quick riches to poverty. It's a universal story and it happens over and over again. When will men learn that what satisfies the hogs won't satisfy us? We were made for better things.

Let me quote to you from the confessions of one young man who savored sin and learned the truth that he couldn't make it on husks:

> What did I really want? Nothing except to love and be loved. But I failed to set up the heart-to-heart relationship that marks the bright trail of friendship. Instead, out of the slimy potholes of flesh and the geysers of puberty there arose vapors that exhaled upon and covered over and obscured my heart, so that I could not tell the blue skies of real love from the polluted overcast of my appetites.
>
> Both were mixed up inside me in confusion and together they lured my immature youth over the precipice of sexual desire and dropped me in a whirlpool of shame and disgrace. . . . I was tossed back and forth, spilling, squandering, and wasting. . . .

That confession has all the earmarks of present-day agony. Actually, it is from Sherwood Wirt's translation of Augustine's confessions. What a pity that each generation must make its own discovery!

FASCINATION

It's a fascinating journey to that far country! No one

denies that. And it's a "riot" after you get there. Whatever you have to spend, there is a place to spend it—your money, your health, your good name, your sensitivity to all that is worthwhile. You can spend all in a hurry, just as the Prodigal did (Luke 15:14).

A nationally known television personality declared to a network audience, "I object to the marriage contract. Love is the strongest and most binding contract of all." It seems thrilling, in the beginning, to leave home and all it stands for—to get away from it all as far as possible. It's exciting to make new discoveries. There's a fascination about the far country.

An Oscar winner who was still reveling in the journey to a far country, said, "I don't think it's desirable to conform . . . [Those who do] go around frustrated most of their lives. . . . But who said that's the natural basic personality of man? To whom does monogamy make sense? To a muskrat, maybe."

She thought her idea was new and daring. But it's all been tried before—so many times. And it always leads to the husks. You arrive at a gnawing, chasmic emptiness.

It's bad enough to lose your money, your health, your friends, your independence, even your self-respect. But to lose your soul is hell. "He would fain have filled his belly with the husks that the swine did eat," Jesus said.

HOG HEAVEN

The Prodigal discovered something shocking the day he looked into the face of a hog and vied with swine for husks. He knew he was a long way from home—a long, long way.

Entrances can be decoys. The excitement of traveling in a far country can have a certain attraction to it.

42

The advertising promises you so much. It promises you a wealth of experience—real adult stuff. Out there in the far country, you'll have an opportunity to do your own thing. You can trample precedent underfoot. You can scorn tradition. You can taste and touch without those hampering rules. There are no inhibitions there: nothing can fence you in. Nothing, that is, but sin's hogpen.

The Prodigal believed that line, until he had fallen so low he looked into the face of a hog and realized how big a tumble he had taken.

I read the glossy pages. I see the bright lights. I hear the sophisticated talk. I look at the veneer of sin. The avenues to those moral hogpens are the best-lighted, most heavily traveled thoroughfares in town. You can hardly wait to pay the fee. You feel you haven't lived until you learn what it's all about.

There is an abundant supply of these "hog heavens" around. Go inside! Look at the merchandise! Examine the wares. Ask yourself what future is there. I'll tell you this. You'll reach for more and more and get less and less. "He would fain have filled his belly with the husks that the swine did eat" (Luke 15:16). That's the test. He wanted to be satisfied with those husks but he couldn't. Where is the satisfaction the world has to offer? It may provide a pacifier for a little while, but the restless hunger for God and what is good and right lurks in the darkness and makes its insistent demands upon the soul.

The far country won't be all you dreamed it would be, when you find yourself competing with the hogs for something to satisfy your craving soul. From the way people talked to you about that far country, you envisioned something a great deal better. They told you that was where you would find your kicks—the real ones.

They didn't tell you about the smell—stale and sour and sweaty. They didn't tell you about the filth —vulgar and cheap and degrading. They didn't tell you about the hopelessness—the murder and divorce and theft and lies. "No man gave unto him" (Luke 15:16).

It's rapacious. It's the jungle. It's mire and muck. You are with hogs—selfish, brutish, rooting for themselves and unconcerned about you or anybody else.

You shouldn't be there at all. You were born for something better. There's a better place to be than draped over a barstool, listening to the swill of a person who hasn't enough presence of mind left to tell you where he lives.

There's a better use for your money than to spend it on that which does not satisfy. There's a better way than coughing, spitting, inhaling smoke, blowing, chewing, and "wasting your substance." There's a nobler use for your body than to fill it with gonorrhea and syphilis or some other social disease that gnaws the life and strength out of you and visits your sins on the next generation. There's a better paradise than that temporary "high" that comes from a needle in your arm. Any way you look at it, there's not much future in romping with hogs in the far country.

The Awful Hunger

The outer wrappings—the showy packaging—the husks of the world don't have the power to sustain. You can't build a marriage or a home on booze. It will rip your marriage apart and take you away from your children and from the companion who finds your drunken antics unbearable.

The hunger for easy winnings at the gambling table is never satisfied. It gnaws and dazzles and tantalizes the soul, and takes the clothes off your back and food off your table, but you stay hungry when you look to gambling for satisfaction. A thousand other vices can tell the same story.

Esau thought he would be satisfied with soup. Judas thought silver would meet all his needs. Ahab sold himself for sex. Demas thirsted for this present world. Cain chose violence. Balaam loved the wages of unrighteousness. Peter tried profanity. Herod chose vulgarity. All of them made the trip into the far country, and for all of them their chief delight turned to husks. The evidence is in. The jury has returned. The verdict is this: "He would fain have filled his belly with the husks that the swine did eat."

I have seen a terrible, insatiable hunger in humanity in my many years as an evangelist. There is the hunger of the lonely for friendship. There is the hunger of the ambitious for success. There is the hunger of the rejected for acceptance. There is the hunger of the slave for freedom. There is the hunger of the unloved for affection.

They seek relief in the bleatings and stammerings of a thousand songs that, in the end, leave them bored and flaccid, wondering what the next song will bring. They dress and bedeck themselves in fashions that mock the soul and mar the image of God in them. They are still wanting. They scrounge and save and protect their mounds of material wealth like squirrels hoarding nuts against a cold winter.

They scramble for tidbits of favor tumbled toward them by some momentary star in the fickle eye of public opinion. They hide in the darkness of the cinema and feed their starving souls on make-believe.

They succor their jaded appetites at the track, the bar, the nightclub, and the beach.

But always there is hunger—pitiful, driving hunger that these husks can never satisfy.

YOU CAN'T MAKE IT ON HUSKS

You can't make it on husks. Jesus met a woman who admitted it. She had been divorced five times. She had thrown off restraint and was living without the drag of a marriage certificate. All that is a matter of record. But something else is also a matter of record. She had a longing that no amount of sex, inside or outside the marriage contract, could satisfy. "Give me . . . that I thirst not, neither come hither to draw," she begged Jesus (John 4:15).

Neither the high nor the low can be satisfied with husks, no matter what the brand or flavor. King Herod found husks at the end of the line after he had scorned all that was good and set himself up as a god.

He came from a family of popularity seekers. They built everything from a temple for the Jews in Jerusalem to political bridges toward the power bases in imperial Rome to sustain their glamour and front-page publicity. They gloried in self-aggrandizement and enjoyed their own images.

But Herod's trip ended unceremoniously. "And upon a set day Herod, arrayed in royal apparel, sat upon his throne, and made an oration. . . . And the people gave a shout, saying, It is the voice of a god, and not of a man. And immediately the angel of the Lord smote him, because he gave not God the glory: and he was eaten of worms, and gave up the ghost" (Acts 12:21-23). It happens still today.

Ask yourself, where are the stars of yesterday? Worms have devoured their short-lived memories.

They are gods one day and ghosts the next. It is said of Ephraim in the Old Testament that he "feedeth on wind" (Hosea 12:1). You are popular one day and a problem the next. Isaiah uses another metaphor: "He feedeth on ashes" (Isaiah 44:20).

Only God knows how many of yesterday's celebrities and how many of those who might have been celebrities are finishing out their days right now in some dingy, forgotten alley of life, feeding on yesterdays, showing their faded newspaper clippings, and knowing inside the emptiness of it all.

The Bible says, "The wicked are like the troubled sea, when it cannot rest, whose waters cast up mire and dirt. There is no peace, saith my God, to the wicked" (Isaiah 57:20, 21).

"The way of peace they know not; and there is no judgment in their goings: they have made them crooked paths: whosoever goeth therein shall not know peace" (Isaiah 59:8).

Wasted years take their toll of wasted opportunities. Years when young people should have been schooled and disciplined and tutored in order to serve their generation and make the world a better place have been tossed away. Sin has convinced them with its challenge, "Have fun while you can. Have your fling. Let tomorrow take care of itself."

And now that tomorrow is here, what can you do that is worthwhile? What have you done with your talents and abilities, given you by God in heaven? Where is your youthful strength, with the personality that was unique to you among all earth's billions? These are the years that the locusts and caterpillars of vain living eat away. There's no shock like the shock of realizing that you have wasted opportunities that may never come again. There's no consternation like that of finding out that you are not in demand any more, that you have been passed up because you yourself passed up the moment of opportunity for something easier.

Business needs something more than the fancy drinker. Government demands more than the carefree shirker. Competition is keen. .

They could have used you back there at home in the beginning. There was a place and a need for your freshness and healthy background, for your good reputation, your potential for advancement, your youthful eagerness. But what have you got to offer now? The market is glutted with worn-out, second-hand lives, spent in the pursuit of pleasure and jaded with the continual round of parties and wasteful living.

The Prodigal's first realization of what his total bill would be came when he realized he had "spent all" and "he began to be in want." He learned how low he had fallen the day a "citizen" of that far country sent him into his field to feed hogs.

THERE'S A WAY OUT

But God in heaven offers every human being an option, however far he has fallen. No man need wallow in the pigpen. No man need keep on being gnawed and clawed by an insatiable hunger —tormented by wrappings—those promises that never deliver—the phantoms and mirages of life. This planet was never intended to be a hogpen or a penitentiary.

I'll tell you this. If you turn your back on the Father—if you waste your substance—if you choose riotous living—you're headed for a famine of the worst kind. This is a famine of the mind and of the soul and of the spirit, for the things that only God in heaven can provide. It's what's in Father's presence that can satisfy you. It's the food in Father's house that can build you up and restore some of those wasted things.

The Prodigal knew about the husks when you left, so full, so free, so self-sufficient. Is this where you are now? Then my message is for you. It has your name and address on it. So take the first step on the long trip back home. Turn around.

The first thing to do is to admit your mistakes. Don't alibi. Don't blame your parents for being too strict with you. Don't blame them for being liberal. You insisted on your portion, remember? And you were in a hurry for it. Place the blame where it belongs—upon your own personal choice.

Notice the Prodigal didn't say, "The devil made me do it." The devil doesn't make anyone do anything. He plants the temptation before us. He dresses the window. But it isn't in his power to make you do it. If that were so, men would be shoved into hell in spite of themselves.

No, the choice is yours, and yours alone. That is why recovery must begin with repentance, with acknowledging your own sin and your terrible need. So take the first step. You were made for something better than competing with hogs for the husks of this world.

When you take that step, heaven will furnish all the encouragement you need to get all the way back home.

5

The Moment of Truth

A newspaperman mistakenly received a letter intended for the wife of an inmate of one of our state penitentiaries. There was no return name on the envelope, only a number and the address of a state penitentiary. The initials and name were the same as the one who should have received the letter. The letter was from a prisoner to his wife, and it told its own poignant story.

I will be getting out of here about the first of December. I am still thinking about you, and still love you, although you told me never to say that anymore.

How are things down that way? How's my little Fred? And Josie? In good shape, I hope, because I surely would feel bad if any one of you was getting along bad on account of me and on account of I'm not there to be of help to you.

I could be of help to you all now 'cause I have no law to hide from like I did when first we married. But things just didn't work out so either of us could be happy, did they?

It was easy to picture the man sitting on an iron cot, struggling over the lines of love that were so hard for him to write.

I'm going to practice the automobile repair trade when I get out. I want to work and work hard, and then when the day is done, I want a home, or a room if nothing better, that I can walk into and clean up. I want to be able to put on a different shirt every night.

You told me once that you weren't giving up on me because you didn't love me, but because I had hurt you and the children so.

Well, I don't want to hurt you anymore but I would like for you to do one thing for me.

I'm coming through home on the bus but I ain't going to stop, because I got a promise of a job in another state where no one knows me and I can make a fresh start. I wish you would bring the children down so I could see them and you. I won't say nothing if you don't want me to, but if you would all like to go on down to that other state with me to live—I'll bet I could find some seats on that bus.

PERSPECTIVE

A moment of truth—when suddenly we see things in their real perspective—is a sobering moment. I have seen it at the moment of execution, when a man stepped into the gas chamber, or mounted the scaffold. I have seen it in colleges at examination time. I have seen it in hospitals when people have been wheeled in for surgery. I have seen it in the debtor's eye as creditors demanded settlements. There is no tomorrow in that moment. The string has run out.

The ugliest part of sin is its deception, the fool it makes of you. Sin makes promises to you that it never can fulfill. There comes a moment when you realize that you have been taken, when you know how Saul felt when he admitted, "I have played the fool, and have erred exceedingly" (1 Samuel 26:21).

The truth is, we never know how good home is until we get away from it. It so often takes loneliness and emptiness to make us homesick. But that moment will come. You will get homesick for God. There'll come a moment when you will get a clearer perspective on things than you have had up until the present.

Do you blame your misery on the poor example of some professing Christians? Have you let them distort your vision? Religious snobbery is hard to take, admittedly. The bar, the casino, the lounge, the nightclub, all seem to offer a greater welcome. But that is deceptive. There is more for you at home in Father's house than you'll ever find in the far country.

Charles Haddon Spurgeon illustrated it this way. A man who owned an apple orchard invited another to eat apples from his orchard. The invitation was repeatedly given and just as often refused. The owner kept insisting until finally the neighbor confided, "To tell you the truth, I have tasted apples from your orchard. As I rode along the other day, I picked up some which had fallen over the fence. Frankly, I never tasted more sour fruit in my life."

To this the owner replied, "Oh, I thought so. You see, the apples on the outside of the orchard are for the special benefit of the boys in the neighborhood. I hunted high and low for trees bearing those sour apples, and when the boys taste them, they give them up as not worth stealing. But come inside the orchard. There you will find the apples sweet and delicious."

The fruit isn't all sour! Give the kingdom of God a chance to prove that to you. Of course, there are imperfect people in the church. "But as many as received him, to them gave he power *to become* the sons of God" (John 1:12). There is a beginning. And there is growth. The promise is "power to become." You have to start some time.

HEADING HOME

One day a gambler walked into my church office. He was finished. Nothing is as pathetic or as revealing as to see a victim of chance turn from a roulette wheel or the poker table, stripped. Everything is gone except a bit of bravado.

It is a lonely moment when you realize you have flung away the decent living that once belonged to you, to your wife and your family. You are finished, spent, bankrupt. There is not even a place at the table for you any longer.

When I looked into that man's face, the words of the Prodigal were written all over it, "I perish with hunger" (Luke 15:17).

Would I try to find his wife and daughter, he wondered. They were living in my city somewhere. Here was the last known address. He thought his wife was doing housework in some rich man's home, trying to earn enough to keep the little girl in school. Would I intercede one more time? He knew now that he had had enough, that he could not win, that there is not something-for-nothing in this world. He would come home and go to work to make a living if she would give him one more chance and believe in him.

I helped that man. I found his family and I promised them a husband and daddy again. What security could I give them? Some of the best security in the world: "And when he came to himself, he said, How many hired servants of my father's have bread enough and to spare, and I perish with hunger." When a man sees himself like that, he's heading home, and God is heading toward the Cross to meet him there.

REAL FREEDOM

Some feel that the church is too restrictive. They have the idea that God's people have a joyless, drab existence, that to be a follower of Christ is to be handcuffed and straitjacketed.

But in Father's house there is "bread enough and to spare." The Father runs a wonderful home. It's not bondage. It's freedom. Jesus Christ told it like it is. "I am the door: by me if any man enter in, he shall be saved, and shall go in and out, and find pasture" (John 10:9). This is glorious freedom.

King David was not a monastic. His testimony concerning service to God was this: "Thou wilt show me the path of life: in thy presence is fulness of joy; at thy right hand there are pleasures for evermore" (Psalm 16:11). That doesn't sound like a restrictive life.

The disciples never complained about lack of excitement or of monotony in Christ's company. They were muscular masculine hunks of humanity. They often went fishing. They ate with colorful celebrities of the day. They mingled with crowds. They knew adventure. The Christ concept is abundant life.

We all get the idea that the rules are too tight before we leave home. It's a different story when you find yourself at loose ends. Then you long for someone to put a little discipline and order into your life. You get tired of sin's problems and the daily mess of disorderly living. It's better to be a servant at home than a son in a far country.

Yet many, grieving in sin and separation, want to come home but are convinced that it is impossible. They feel sure they could never change.

The question they ask isn't whether or not Christianity is real. They know it is. The question they ask is, "Is it possible for me to be a Christian?" They wonder, "Were I to come home to Father's house, would I be accepted?" They ask, "Could I be changed?" The uncertainty keeps many from starting home.

GOD'S FIRST NAME

Acceptance starts with repentance. "I have sinned . . . and am no more worthy" (Luke 15:18, 19). Christ offers a carte blanche. "Him that cometh to me I will in no wise cast out" (John 6:37). You have been issued a credit card. Use it! Christ sees the potential, as yet unrealized, in you. And you love Him for that faith He exercises toward you. It makes you try all the harder.

Here is a music teacher with extremely high standards of musical perfection. He asks from the pupil so many hours of practice and requires measurable progress. It can make for a stern and strained relationship. The pupil can give up, overwhelmed by the unattainable standard of perfection. He might be tempted to abandon music altogether for this reason. Certainly he would find it difficult to love the teacher.

But there is a different potential. Let us see a teacher reaching out in love to help a pupil distressed and discouraged by his very obvious limitations. That pupil can respond to the faith the teacher is exercising toward him. Yes, the teacher will have high standards. He could not redeem if it were otherwise. The pupil knows it. So he tries—but without condemnation. That is the crucial point. He knows the teacher is helping him and demanding better of him because he loves him.

God's first name is Love.

Paul told the Roman believers, "Yea, he shall be holden up: for God is able to make him stand" (Romans 14:4). Count on that grace and come home!

A Better Deal

Success or failure in Christian living is determined by how much we allow God to love us, and by how much we love Him. Progress stops and disaster begins when we stop trusting. Trust Him! He is both "the author and the finisher of our faith" (Hebrews 12:2). What He promises, He is able to perform. Our salvation comes with a full warranty: "I can do all things through Christ which strengtheneth me" (Philippians 4:13). So, come home!

Something tells you there is a better deal in Father's house than anywhere else in the world. "How many hired servants of my father's have bread enough and to spare, and I perish with hunger!"

Once you heard the voice of ambition—coaxing, persuasive, tantalizing. It was real. It told you that if you would leave home, leave the familiar, leave the old values, get away from your early training, you would be on your way to success. You could go a long way in this world if you could break the old restraints. You could spend freely, because you would have plenty. You could do as you pleased, and it would be nobody's business but your own.

Now hear another voice. It is an honest voice. It is full of love. It has survived the squalor and failure that marred your ambitious trip to the far country. It reaches past the waste and the famine and the hurts and the husks. Its message is plain: "Come home! You belong here. I will forgive. I will clothe. I will provide. I will love. I will not forsake."

The first voice seduced then abandoned you. The voice of your Heavenly Father is warm with anxiety, and it never promises what it can't deliver. It breathes assurance. It speaks with a compassion that can't be found in the company of swine.

Let your homesickness turn you around and start you toward Father's house. Consider the possibilities of a better life at home than you ever found in that far country, then act on what you know to be true.

6
Bold Resolution

The man or woman who looks around as the Prodigal did and realizes where he is, is in an excellent position to resolve to start out for something better. That person knows some action is required on his part if his circumstances are ever going to change.

You can drift into a lost eternity; but you cannot drift into heaven. Heaven is by appointment only.

You must want to go to heaven and do something about it as surely as you want to arise in the morning and dress and eat. You must choose where you will spend your hereafter as deliberately as you choose where to go when you get into your automobile and start the engine.

You can feed on the "husks that the swine did eat" or you can sit at the Father's table and take your place as a son. It's up to you. No church can make that decision for you. No preacher can. No praying loved one can. That responsibility—and privilege—is yours alone. The church will open its doors. The preacher will extend the invitation. Loved ones and friends will weep for you, but the bold resolution to "arise and go to my Father" is yours. No one denied you the choice when you left. No one denies you the decision to come home.

And it shouldn't be too hard to make up your mind to come home with all the help God furnishes you.

First, God provides conscience for all of us. That is the law of God written in our hearts. It is the "umpire" in a man's soul. John speaks of it as "the light that lighteth every man that cometh into the world. . . ." You must reckon with your own conscience, that inner light that points out the difference between what is right and what is wrong. That's a basic incentive that God in His mercy provides.

Second, God provides the Bible. What is right and what is wrong are written down in black and white. It's the Rule Book. History records that when nations honor God and His Word, God honors them. When nations dishonor God and violate His Word, they themselves are dishonored. The same holds true for individuals.

You don't have to be a preacher to tell how these rules work. Germany demonstrated for the whole world in this century that these rules cannot be broken without the rules breaking the transgressor. Other nations have learned the same bitter lesson. It doesn't matter who you are, the Rule Book—the Bible—applies to you. It applies to us all. Whether we think so or not is incidental. The Book is bigger than we are. That's the second incentive God provides.

Third, God provides His Son. Jesus Christ is a fact, not a myth. He is a part of mankind. His claim upon the human race is indisputable. What other rational explanation can be found for His life, death, and resurrection, than his work of atonement? The simple answer is this: What He did He did for me. What He did He did for you. He gave this world the hope of the gospel. You cannot have the gospel without Christ. They are inseparable. That's the third incentive God provides for your decision. And there are more.

Fourth, God is in charge of circumstances. What happens to us is not simply good or bad luck. We are not the playthings of blind, unreasonable fate. We are not at the mercy of the stars. It isn't tea leaves or the crystal ball. No! Your circumstances are in the hands of God. He has intervened for you when you wouldn't and couldn't have saved yourself. He has spoken to you by narrow escape—a rescue that seemed impossible—a recovery that puzzled the physician—a profit that seemed altogether unlikely. Many have never thanked God for these things. They act as though they alone were responsible. They are quick to curse Him for their losses. But deep, deep inside they know that an Almighty Hand reaches out to them in love. That love calls us to God.

Fifth, God provides the Holy Spirit. He alone holds back the corruption and moral rebellion of this world. Mankind would be worse than he is if it were not for the presence of the Holy Spirit in the world. He brings to you the memory of a parent's prayer for your salvation. He reminds you of former days when you served the Lord. He brings to mind golden texts you learned in Sunday school. He nudges you about promises you have volunteered when you were in tight spots. God's Spirit deals with you when no preacher can reach you. You may have given up going to church entirely, but you can't get away from the Holy Spirit. You may barricade your life against Him; but He lingers with you in love and intercedes for you through the prayers of God's people.

HOW MUCH DO YOU WANT HEAVEN?

God does all of this and more for you every day. Can

you then say that heaven does not want you? The question is, how much do you want heaven—how willing are you to draw nigh to God? I know this to be a fact, " . . . the Lord is . . . not willing that any should perish, but that all should come to repentance. . . . " Hell is the sinner's choice, not God's choice for him.

Christ wept over Jerusalem, that blinded, rejecting city, and pleaded, "Oh . . . how often would I have gathered thy children together and ye would not. . . . " It's your life. You can bless it with virtue or blast it with vice. But don't blame God for what happens. The Prodigal resolved to "arise and go. . . . " That's an option God keeps open for every man. That's the pledge of Calvary. You don't need to stay in the gutter. God says so. God hasn't run away from you. You have run away from God. You may have reached the end of the line, but the road back is open. You can ignore it, or resolve to start home.

WHY DO YOU WAIT?

Do you hesitate because you do not feel your need of Christ? You are moral and manly. Your honor and reputation are unquestioned. You are willing to compare your life with that of any professing Christian in town. People who do this remind me of the difference between mineral and vegetable, between a piece of lovely quartz and an acorn. It is not hard to choose between the two when compared on the outside. The shining beauty of the mineral easily overshadows the acorn. But the acorn has something on the inside that the quartz doesn't have. The acorn has life. The quartz has reached the ultimate of possibilities. The acorn has just begun. That's a true picture of the difference between natural goodness and spiritual life.

Morality reaches its highest development upon

earth in culture, refinement, charity. All that is human progress. It sparkles. It attracts attention, even commendation. It is beautiful. But it is dead, lifeless, mechanical, without Jesus. There is no inward, eternal life without Him. He that hath the Son hath life; but he that hath not the Son, shall not see life, but the wrath of God abideth on him."

A baseball pitcher may throw a straight or curved pitch. A curve depends upon the spiral motion given to the ball as it leaves the pitcher's hand. It is possible for a pitcher to so conceal this motion that both pitches appear alike until they reach the strike zone. Only then will they differ. Life is like that. Two men may seem to be traveling in the same direction. There seems to be no apparent difference in their lives. Outwardly they are both gentlemen—respectable and industrious. But inside there's a difference. There is that motion, concealed from sight, that will finally take one away from God—swerve him away from heaven and turn him in an altogether different direction. It's what happens finally that counts.

What is the inner motion of your heart? Head and hand may appear to be in control of the situation, but what about your heart? Not without significance are the words of the wise man, "Keep thy heart with all diligence; for out of it are the issues of life" (Proverbs 4:23). Is your heart bent toward God? That is the crucial question.

You say, "I haven't enough feeling about it to take action." Let me ask you, "How much steam does an engine need?" Just enough to turn the machinery and propel the wheels. How much feeling must a man have to resolve to turn in the right direction? Just enough to start. All the feeling you need to make you want to be a Christian is to see the rottenness of this world system, to feel how hollow it is. The taste of husks and the smell of pigs gave the Prodigal all the feeling he needed to turn him around and start him back home where he knew things were infinitely better even for the servants.

DON'T LOSE BY DEFAULT!

You ought to turn around now. Indecision is fatal. Hardly a lost soul ever chose to be lost. They are eternal losers by default—by neglect. Every time you postpone this matter, your power to decide weakens.

Suppose I take a magnet and hold it over some tacks. See how they cling! The magnet draws them easily. And here are some of the larger ones—but not as many leap to the magnet. And here are some shingle nails, but only a few. And even fewer six- and eight-penny nails respond to the influence of the magnet. And when you come to the spike, one end may drag along, but no amount of coaxing or hovering over it with the magnet will lift it.

So it is with the grace of God! The youngsters come to God easily; growing boys and girls find it a little harder. With every added year the weight of sin and guilt increases, and it becomes harder for the soul to respond to the grace of God that calls the soul heavenward. Childhood is the open door. Youth is the closing gateway. Manhood is a barricaded entrance. But if we stir ourselves and resolve to go, drawn by His grace, what a welcome awaits us!

Insurance companies work on actuary tables. These are tables of probabilities and possibilities. These calculations leave little opportunity for chance. Likewise, the Church has observed over centuries of gospel-preaching similar equations. Are you nearing the age of 21? If you have not yet decided for Christ, the chances are one in three that you will. Have you passed the age of 25 without having made the bold resolution to come to God in response to His call? According to the sternest arithmetic, the chances are ten to one that you will be lost forever. Yet God was not willing that any should perish. It is easier to turn toward God in this moment than it ever will be again for you, because every decision you make to postpone the greatest decision of all makes it harder to change direction.

There are pivotal moments in every man's life —moments when risk and opportunity seem to culminate. These are hours when we stand at the crossroads, when fortunes are made or lost. But the most momentous hour on earth for anyone is that hour when God reaches out and makes him know—as he may never again quite as fully know—that He wants that person, that He is striving for him.

Aaron Burr met such an hour when, in a New England village, a faithful servant of God presented Jesus to him. For hours afterward, it is said, Aaron Burr paced the floor of his room. It was long past midnight when he finally looked out his window toward the stars and bade God good-bye. He determined to live from that time on only to fulfill his personal ambitions. And from that moment on, his long career became a story of increasing shame and ignominy. He made the choice that took him away from God.

IT'S YOUR MOVE

But the prodigal can turn homeward. He has a standing invitation. No man need go "hungry" in soul, be morally bankrupt, be in want, or get as low as the pigs. A man can "come to himself" and say, "I will arise and go to my father, and will say unto him, Father, I have sinned against heaven, and before thee." A man can say that, and then start on his way back!

Here is what the Bible says, "If we confess our sins, he is faithful and just to forgive us our sins, and to cleanse us from all unrighteousness." And the Bible also says, "Him that cometh unto me, I will in no wise cast out."

Are you sick of your sin? If you are not, then let me tell you that sin is one commodity of which you can have all you want. If you don't get enough on this side of the grave, there will be a whole eternity full of it. You can have all the sin you crave! But God waits for you to turn away from your sin. He waits for you to weary of it, to resent its heavy burden, to despise your taskmaster, to hate your vile and wicked habits, to once more long for moral purity and fellowship with the Father. Many a lost one has started on the road back and made it because he knew the Father was waiting for him.

The next move is yours. You must say for yourself, "I will arise and go to my Father. . . . " Everything eternal in your life waits on that decision.

7
Does Anybody Care?

We don't know much about the Prodigal's journey home, but his thoughts must have dwelt on how little he was taking home after starting out with so much. He had a plan, though. He was going to ask to be made as the hired servants. His father's grace had not yet been revealed to him in its fullness.

But "when he was yet a great way off, his father saw him, and had compassion, and ran, and fell on his neck, and kissed him" (Luke 15:20).

If you cannot accept the grace of God, this message has no interest for you. All of us are "a great way off"—the best of us as well as the worst of us. It could be discouraging, but we'll never make it home without help—a lot of it.

THE LONG WAY HOME

During World War I, thousands of homesick men sang, "There's a long, long trail awinding into the land of my dreams." And it's a long, long trail for us toward God's paradise—a long one even after we make the decision to "arise and go" to our Father.

No one started farther back on that trail than David did. I believe Luke 15:20 can apply to David's life. If

God ever had compassion—if He ever "ran" toward anyone stumbling forward, often crawling, toward home—it was toward David.

First, God ran toward David when he was a nobody in the back pasture. The boy was so far back that no one invited him to the meeting with Samuel. "And Samuel said unto Jesse, Are here all thy children? And he said, There remaineth yet the youngest, and, behold, he keepeth the sheep. And Samuel said unto Jesse, Send and fetch him: for we will not sit down till he come hither" (1 Samuel 16:11).

God looked farther than the preacher or the elder. He saw what they did not see. He saw a teenager—a guitar-picking, ballad-composing, long-haired teenager, whose stories about killing lions and bears raised as many eyebrows among the older folk as Joseph, dressed in his loud sports jacket, had raised among the adults about his recurring dreams. But in looking past the exterior, God saw faith. "For the Lord seeth not as man seeth; for man looketh on the outward appearance, but the Lord looketh on the heart" (1 Samuel 16:7).

It takes "heart" to start in the right direction, because no one—except God—believes you can travel all that long, long trail back home. So few folk reach toward a kid to pat him on the back, and say, "You'll make it! I know you will." More of us ought to do it more often.

God is doing it all the time. He did it for Jacob, when the whole neighborhood would have written him off as a cheat and a scoundrel.

He did it for Gideon, a backward boy who knew his own discouraging reputation and deplored it. "My family is poor . . . and I am the least in my father's house" (Judges 6:15).

He did it for Mark when Paul wrote him off as a bad risk. God knows how many teenagers are "a great way off" today, and God is still the God of "compassion" who "runs" toward them.

GOD RUNS TO MEET YOU

Second, God ran toward David when he dared to tackle Goliath. No one was as green, as inexperienced as this country bumpkin. His military brothers scorned him. They were irritated and embarrassed by his presence. "Why camest thou down hither?" they wanted to know. "And with whom hast thou left those few sheep in the wilderness?" (1 Samuel 17:28).

David didn't look like a soldier. He didn't act like one. He was "a great way off." It seemed the most unequal contest in history—a bantam versus a heavyweight, a slingshot versus shield, spear, sword, and armor—a professional against an amateur. Goliath could have obtained odds of 200 to one easily, even among the Israelis that day. "And when the Philistine looked about, and saw David, he disdained him: for he was but a youth" (1 Samuel 17:42).

It would be a long, long way to the throne, but that "youth" was headed in that direction. "I come to thee in the name of the Lord of hosts. . . . This day will the Lord deliver thee into mine hand" (1 Samuel 17:45, 46).

God ran toward David faster than the giant could stride toward the country boy. That was the day the Heavenly Father "kissed" him. The headlines roared the story. "And David took the head of the Philistine, and brought it to Jerusalem; but he put his armor in his tent" (1 Samuel 17:54).

After it is all over, a lot of folk who a few hours before wanted to kick you, are the first in line wanting to *kiss* you. But it's when you're "a great way off" that you need encouragement. Anybody can congratulate a winner. God is reaching out to people who look like losers, folk the experts agree will never make it. Remember how He went to meet Peter when most religious authorities would have expelled him indefinitely!

He found Elijah when the evangelist was so discouraged he wanted to die. He forgave a woman when critics were ready to stone her, and He said to her, "Neither do I condemn thee" (John 8:11). Just make a start in the right direction, and you'll have company all the way.

Third, God ran toward David when he had the Cave of Adullam as his headquarters and 400 ragamuffin soldiers as his army. You would have to say that he was still "a great way off."

It looked like a City Union Mission more than it looked like a cathedral. "And every one that was in distress, and every one that was in debt, and every one that was discontented, gathered themselves unto him; and he became captain over them: and there were with him about four hundred men" (1 Samuel 22:2).

It didn't seem to be much of a congregation. You couldn't have raised much money. There was more grumbling than there was get-up-and-go. But you can go a long way if there is compassion.

Poor beginnings have provided many a world leader. A Bethlehem manger gave us the Saviour. An Egyptian penitentiary gave us Joseph. House arrest gave us the Pauline Epistles. Exile gave us Nehemiah. Outcast society gave us Matthew. Army life gave us Cornelius.

I love those words in this verse: " . . . and had compassion." God cares about you. It doesn't take a bank account. It doesn't take a smart uniform. It doesn't take a grade card with straight "A's" to make it. You've got a long piece of road ahead of you, but God says, "My grace is sufficient for you." With that grace you can make it all the way home.

People have made it with a lot less than David had, because of God's grace. The choice to accept that grace and appropriate it for your need is up to you. The grace and its unfailing supply is up to God.

Fourth, God ran toward David when he sought refuge and understanding among the Philistines. David seemed to be fighting for a national cause that no one really cared about. He was like an Old Testament Don Quixote. "And David said in his heart, I shall now perish one day by the hand of Saul: there is nothing better for me than that I should speedily escape into the land of the Philistines" (1 Samuel 27:1).

It was the low point in the shepherd's biography. He felt no one cared. His life had been fragmented. There was a price on his head. Bad water and hard rations had dulled the dreams of palace and crown.

The same temptation hit him that hits us all: "With friends like these, who needs enemies?"

You ache for the warrior as he grovels before the Philistines. "If I have now found grace in thine eyes, let them give me a place in some town in the country" (1 Samuel 27:5).

But David's story did not end on that note. In that moment he was wide open for demolition. The Philistines never had a better chance. But "the father . . . fell on him." God covered him, or there

69

would have been no more David. No wonder that he sang later, "He shall cover thee with his feathers, and under his wings shalt thou trust: his truth shall be thy shield and buckler" (Psalm 91:4).

The Philistine said, "He hath made his people Israel utterly to abhor him; therefore he shall be my servant for ever" (1 Samuel 27:12). But God had other plans for David.

Fifth, God ran toward him—after he finally became king—when he lost all sense of self-control and shamed his God, his nation, and his family. In that moment it looked as though David had dropped out of sight. He was a rake, a murderer, an alienator of affections, a liar, a miserable spiritual dropout. You can hear his agony all the way from the 51st Psalm: "I acknowledge my transgressions: and my sin is ever before me. . . . Behold, I was shapen in iniquity; and in sin did my mother conceive me" (vv. 3, 5).

No man in history has stood more battered by sin's assault. The smell of the pigpen permeated the palace. A cheapness that men in the ranks would have spurned had infiltrated the high command. It was a rotten affair from start to finish. Bathsheba had reduced a king to a fool in a matter of minutes. It was a wrong turn that led to multiplied sorrows.

GOD SEES A LONG WAY

But "his father saw him." David lived to thank God for that. His Father saw him as he "walked upon the roof . . . and from the roof he saw a woman washing herself" (2 Samuel 11:2). His Father saw him as "he inquired after the woman" (2 Samuel 11:3). His Father saw him as he made arrangements with General Joab for her husband's death.

"His father *saw* him." Count on that! He watches

70

every assault of hell upon his children. And He "ran" toward David. God didn't lose any time. The preacher was there before the marriage license. "And the Lord sent Nathan unto David. . . . And Nathan said to David, Thou are the man. . . . And David said unto Nathan, I have sinned against the Lord" (2 Samuel 12:1, 7, 13).

And then there is the word of forgiveness, "The Lord also hath put away thy sin; thou shalt not die" (2 Samuel 12:13).

Finally, God ran toward David when he presumed in his own wisdom to number the people. Joab, the old leatherneck, knew better. He said, "But why doth my lord the king delight in this thing?" (2 Samuel 24:3).

David was moving toward the same quicksand, the same trap that swallowed Nebuchadnezzar when "he walked in the palace of the kingdom of Babylon . . . (and) spake, and said, Is not this great Babylon, that I have built for the house of the kingdom by the might of my power, and for the honor of my majesty?" (Daniel 4:29, 30).

A lot of "I" and "my" and "me" and "mine" are written in history, a lot of bragging—all displays of pomp and pride. But God resisteth the proud. Count on it. Start on that route, and you'll meet opposition you can't handle. You can't make it without God's help.

Perhaps it's easier to trust God when you are a kid facing a giant than when you are a king with the most assets the nation ever had at your command. A veteran needs God just as much and just as often as a rookie, even if in different ways. Strength is not in numbers. Strength is in God. David had to know that the same God that had set him up could just as easily and just as surely set him aside.

It's a long, long route from the new birth to the New Jerusalem. So this text fits us all, "when he was yet a great way off. . . . " The encouraging part is that from that great distance, "his father saw him and ran," not away from him but toward him.

The fact is if you head toward God and Home, you'll have all the help you need to make it. Start home, and you will feel as though someone is tugging you forward.

The Prodigal had man's company on his way to the far country; but he had God's company on the return trip. Earthly friends flocked around him to help spend his money and to share in riotous living. They had already forsaken him when he landed in the pigpen. But the father saw him when he was yet a great way off, still in rags and in want. And the Father ran toward him. A God like that cares, and He's the God to serve!

8
New Shoes

The questions are often raised concerning the person who has been forgiven, "How far can he go? What strength does he have? Will he make it?"

He will. God intends for him to make it—all the way. "Yea, he shall be holden up: for God is able to make him stand" (Romans 14:4). He is "the author and finisher of our faith" (Hebrews 12:2). "Faithful is he that calleth you, who also will do it" (1 Thessalonians 5:24).

The Prodigal's father did a great deal more than welcome his long-lost son home. He called for a robe for his back and a ring for his hand and shoes for his feet.

PROPERLY CLOTHED

The redemptive act of God in the Garden of Eden provided proper attire for Adam and Eve. "Unto Adam also and to his wife did the Lord God make coats of skins, and clothed them" (Genesis 3:21). Their skimpy attire of "leaves," that would fade and crumble, could never pass divine inspection. For "they sewed fig leaves together, and made themselves aprons" (Genesis 3:7). You need more than an "apron" to please God. You need a "robe." You need something that Blood has provided, rather than something that nature has grown.

Your righteousness will never do. "Our righteousnesses are as filthy rags" (Isaiah 64:6) in God's sight. Morality can never be a substitute for faith in the Atonement. Ethics can never take the place of redemption. Jesus Christ is "made" unto righteousness. You had better let the Heavenly Father fit you out instead of someone purporting to know what He demands, without the backing of the Word.

Come to God and He will dress you for this world and the world to come. You'll be respected by angels. He clothed a demoniac with sanity. He took an embezzler, Zacchaeus, and clothed him with liberality. He took a prostitute, Mary Magdalene, and clothed her with virtue and made her respectable. He took tempers that made John and James hotheads and clothed them with patience and love. He took a brutish Roman executioner and clothed him with reverence and faith. He took a profane tongue and clothed it with the utterance of the Holy Spirit on the Day of Pentecost.

And he'll take your shame and clothe you with the garments of praise. His victory is to take the prodigals of this world—the wasters, the rebels—and welcome them, and forgive them, and clothe them with His own righteousness. "And of his fulness have all we received, and grace for grace" (John 1:16).

There isn't anything cheap about your Heavenly Father. But there is about the devil. Satan will outfumble you every time for the check. He's never paid anyone's expense in his entire career. The divorcee pays for her own grief. The gambler pays for his own sorrow. The thief pays for his own crime. Lucifer is a

74

mean, cheap boss to work for, and "The way of the transgressor is hard."

But Christ picks up the expense tab on your behalf. "He hath borne our griefs, and carried our sorrows . . . he was wounded for our transgressions, he was bruised for our iniquities: the chastisement of our peace was upon him; and with his stripes we are healed" (Isaiah 53:4, 5). That's a provision that comes once in a lifetime. God offers us His best.

There is nothing stronger than Calvary. There is nothing better than heaven. There is nothing more sure than the Resurrection. There is no one more helpful than the Holy Spirit. There is nothing sweeter than a Christian home. There is nothing truer than the Bible. And all these can be yours when you come to Christ.

SHOES ON HIS FEET

Salvation has *shoes* for the feet. The new birth is a birth into a new society. An emaciated prodigal comes stumbling away from swine, marked by poverty of morals and self-respect, toward the Father, and instantly he becomes, upon confession of faith, the finest security risk this side the throne of God. Certainly, it is a miracle! The power of God is unlimited.

General Ralph E. Haines, West Point graduate and Commanding General, U.S. Continental Army Command, wore these same "shoes" as he witnessed for Christ. In an address at West Point, he told this story: One day at lunch he received an attractive job offer from the representative of a large corporation with a somewhat questionable reputation, and he refused to accept.

The person making the offer was surprised by the refusal and asked for an explanation. The General explained, "I am a man of faith, and I try to do business in accordance with the highest ethical principles. In the light of that, I can see no way to accept your offer."

The man making the offer looked at him across the table and said, "Surely you don't try to mix business and religion!"

The man of faith looked back without flinching and uttered a truth that is meaningful to all Christians. "My friend," he said. "I have discovered that it is only when we do mix business with religion that we can prove our religion and improve our business."

General Haines told the Cadets, "A commitment to Christ is an intensely personal experience. A continual awareness that we have surrendered our lives to Christ and have found the secret of victorious living constitutes the cornerstone of our faith. It is this bedrock truth on which we can fall back and regroup our forces when we are assailed by the turmoil and tribulations of the world."

That General leaves tracks that none can mistake. God put shoes of faith on his feet.

"Put . . . shoes on his feet." You are not wallowing with swine. You are not limping with hunger. You are not humiliated with rags any longer. You are no longer despised. You walk like a man when you are fitted with divinely ordered shoes. David said, "Order my steps in thy word" (Psalm 119:133). When you live like that, each step you take is authorized.

I know those shoes. They are the most comfortable, the longest wearing, and have the greatest built-in support of any shoes available. Paul calls them, "the preparation of the gospel of peace" (Ephesians 6:15).

They took Paul from Jerusalem to Rome, by way of Antioch, Ephesus, Philippi, Corinth, and Athens. He stood on Mars' Hill. He stood before Nero. He stood before mobs. He stood on storm-tossed decks. He stood before death and disease. He stood before persecutor and informer. He stood in prisons. He stood in palaces. And he never lost his footing. He knew where he was going at all times.

There was never a moment of doubt. No uncertainty tripped him. He walked through Asia and Europe as no man ever walked. You ask, "How?" Look at his "shoes!"

Those "shoes" will take you farther and faster than any footwear a world system offers. Paul said, "I therefore so run, not as uncertainly . . . " (1 Corinthians 9:26). Those shoes have a grip that makes you a champion. The gospel will support you in every test. There's an assurance, a deep, settled peace, a know-so that clings, and never lets a man down. It will take you all the way.

You name it, and a child of God has been there. A Livingstone to Africa, a Gilmour to Mongolia, a Judson to Burma, a Grenfell to Labrador, a Simpson and a Plymire to Tibet, a Morrison to China—they have walked and no man could hinder. God "put . . . shoes on [their] feet."

THE ROAD AHEAD

God put shoes on the feet of Israel. For 40 years they tramped the desert, took the heat, wandered in the wilderness of Sinai, and not one sandal showed signs of wear.

Here's the argument that defeats all the sneers of hell. There are members of the human race who walk daily in the midst of evil in a holy manner. They are described by the writer to the Hebrews as people "of whom the world was not worthy" (Hebrews

11:38)—moral heroes and heroines—giants of faith. They forever put the lie to the complaint, "I would like to do it, but I'm afraid I couldn't stand."

You can stand, when you walk in another's "shoes." You need His shoes as much as you need His robe to cover you, and you need His ring to identify you.

Yes, there's a walk ahead of you—a course marked out for you. Salvation is an everyday walk. "For now is our salvation nearer than when we believed" (Romans 13:11). "But he that shall endure unto the end, the same shall be saved" (Matthew 24:13). Your *walk* is as important as your *welcome*.

Hell offers no shoes for the sinner. You'll know that before "many days." The going gets tough and lonely fast. You'll lose the spring in your step. The confident stride disappears. The sense of direction is lost. Suddenly you have an ache that can't be satisfied. Hell makes you a stumblebum.

You need more than a charity-scrap from a "citizen." You need more than endless tomorrows feeding "swine." You need an underfooting that restores dignity and manhood. "Put shoes on his feet," the Father says.

I have this confidence that "he which hath begun a good work in you will perform it until the day of Jesus Christ" (Philippians 1:6). There are "shoes" as well as "shed tears" to the gospel. "And being fully persuaded, that what he had promised, he was also able to perform" (Romans 4:21). Multiplied millions have proved the validity of this persuasion.

In our childhood years we used to read about seven-league boots—the stride of a conqueror. God fits His children at birth with that kind of spiritual footwear. "Nay, in all these things we are more than conquerors through Him that loved us" (Romans 8:37).

John the Baptist knew this kind of victory when he would not flinch before Herod. Stephen would not compromise with the establishment. Peter strode out of a purely kosher and ceremonial world toward the house of Cornelius, and the Gentile was welcomed.

Matthew left the tables of arithmetic and finance and strode toward an Upper Room and a personal Pentecost. Mark found a footing that gave him a base upon which to write the second Gospel narrative. Mary outdistanced seven demons and reached the Resurrection garden in record time. None of them could have made it without the "shoes" the Father provides.

David forever praised God for the strength he found. "He brought me up also out of an horrible pit, out of the miry clay, and set my feet upon a rock, and established my goings" (Psalm 40:2).

"For thou hast delivered my soul from death: wilt not thou deliver my feet from falling, that I may walk before God in the light of the living?" (Psalm 56:13). "Our feet shall stand within thy gates, O Jersualem" (Psalm 122:2). God knows what it will take for the journey.

You won't make it far in your own strength. The trail is too rugged for the barefooted. This isn't the soft mud of a pigpen. This isn't the languor of the far country. This is a climb all the way.

You'll have to quickly move past the jealousies, the grumblings, the accusations, the snubs of the self-righteous. There's no stopping. You'll have to press forward every day. You'll falter without "shoes." The bleeding, the cracks, the fractures, the sprains, the pricks, the infection will stop you without shoes long before you reach your goal.

First, then, thank Him for His compassion, His kiss of pardon. Thank Him for the robe of righteousness and the ring of identification. Then thank Him for "shoes" for the road ahead.

9
They Began to Be Merry

When the Prodigal Son came home, it wasn't long before "they began to be merry" around the old home place. Whatever the date of a prodigal's return, it's just like Christmas for someone who's been waiting for that day.

I have a Christmas list that doesn't appear in the show windows of our stores, and it isn't cataloged by any of the giant mail-order firms of this country. It's a list of gifts that people want more than they want any appliance or any toy that could be wrapped in the glitter of the holiday season. Let me mention a few items on that list—items that could make any day of the year a Christmas for somebody.

GIFTS WITHOUT PACKAGES

Many a little tot wants its daddy more than any gift. You ran away, you deserted a year ago, two years ago, or maybe five. You haven't seen those little kiddies of yours, and they haven't seen you, except to look at your picture, and to say night after night as your wife tucks them into bed, "Mother, why doesn't our Daddy come home to us?" In my years as a radio preacher, the letters that have reached my desk would break the heart of an angel. A lonely mother wrote—a heroic woman, trying her best to keep a home together for the children—asking, "Am I right to keep on encouraging the children when they say their prayers to ask Jesus to send Daddy back to us?"

What would you tell her? Somewhere a man running from God held Christmas for that precious little family in the palm of his sinful hands, in the center of his rebellious heart. In the far country, this prodigal needed to reassess his situation and arise and go home.

Yes, high on that family's list was a gift that only a wayward father could produce. If this shoe fits you, you too can go back to your family and bring the joy that's like Christmas. You've been a prodigal husband and father too long. May God stir longings in your soul out there in that "far country" and bring you home.

The next gift on the list is for parents who would like to hear from sons and daughters. First it was carelessness or rebellion, and now it has become shame that keeps you from letting anxious parents know where you are and whether you are dead or alive. For countless parents in this country today, the greatest and most treasured gift they could receive would be a letter or telephone call from some prodigal son or daughter.

Not even all the diamonds in that store down the street could begin to have the excitement for your parents that your phone call would have. Think of the joy in the heart of the Prodigal's father when he said, "This my son was dead, and is alive again; he was lost, and is found" (Luke 15:24). No wonder they "began to be merry."

What handsome gifts we could give each other!

What power is ours to cause other hearts to begin to be merry! The nagging, complaining wife could give her home and household a brand-new disposition, and it would be more appreciated than the finest gift she could buy for them.

The wise man said in Proverbs 27:15, "A continual dropping in a very rainy day and a contentious woman are alike." Wouldn't it be wonderful to change that whine and complaining for a song and a smile? When other gifts have been forgotten; when pretty things have been washed and faded; when furniture once new sags and is threadbare; when candies have been eaten and flowers withered, the gift of a new disposition will still sparkle and lift the heart.

The miserly husband could give to his family a new spirit of liberality. Many a household Scrooge needs the miracle of Christmas to erase the wrinkles of his dwarfish soul. There are women who would openly weep were their husbands to put an extra five-dollar bill in their hands over and above the household money.

Why have you let your child grow up to think of you as a cold, suspicious banker instead of a big-hearted, loving father? Do you love your money more than you do your child?

Church members hold in their power the gift of encouragement to the pastor—and only God knows how many other persons—just by their faithful presence in the house of God. What wouldn't it do for a pastor's heart if the Sunday morning crowd suddenly turned out for the midweek service! Besides, this would be a gift to yourself as well.

> Where would I be on prayer meeting night,
> If my Lord should suddenly come?
> At church, in my place, or out with the crowd,
> Just having some innocent fun?

Where would I be? Getting food for my soul,
And praying for those who are lost;
Or absent again—forgetting the One
Who bought us at infinite cost?

Where would I be? I've excuse enough,
But how would they look in His sight?
Where would I want Him to find me at last?
Should He come on prayer meeting night?

The list of things that would make sad hearts "begin to be merry" seems to grow as we think about it.

CHECK THE LIST

Let's check our potential gift list. Let's see what we have given during this past year. Employer, could you show a little more courtesy and kindness toward your employee? Employee, have you decided to give an honest effort—to share the concern of your employer about the success of his business? These gifts may not be tied with red ribbon and packaged in cellophane, but they are more valuable to the recipients than turkeys and pen and pencil sets.

People on the verge of divorce are people in pain and distress. If these words find you there this moment, let me challenge you. Your once warm relationship is in shambles. Bitter, angry words have cut it to ribbons, and frightened your children. Resentment has taken all the joy out of life. Your marriage has become a contest instead of a covenant.

Whatever the calendar says, you need a real Christmas in a hurry. Let me suggest that you stop fighting for a moment. Stand together once more by the bed of that child of yours who has cried herself to sleep this day because the big gifts you could have given from your hearts you haven't given—gifts of love and faith and forbearance and understanding.

Stand there and ask yourselves, "Doesn't this wonderful child God sent into our home need a real daddy and a real mother?" Is there any difference of opinion, any selfish desire, of greater importance than the reward that awaits you to have that child some day tell her children, "I had the best mother and daddy in all the world"?

And here is a valid question: "What have you given your own soul?" Once in a while I hear someone say, "This year I gave myself a present." Have you done that—ever? What kind of present? What are the measurements of your soul? What will bring your soul the peace it longs for? What can lift the heavy load? What can silence the accusing voice? What can cancel the past? What can give you rest at night? What can make you live again? Did you find the answer in any one of the packages with your name on them under the tree last Christmas?

THERE'S ANOTHER TREE

If questions like this cause you pain and concern, you need to look under another tree for the present you need most. I can assure you there is a package there with your name on it. And it's paid for. The One who purchased it for you loves you more than anyone you have ever known in all your life. Read the tag on His gift to you, nailed to an old rugged cross for your sins. Here's what it says:

"Come unto me, all ye that labor and are heavy laden, and I will give you rest. Take my yoke upon you, and learn of me; for I am meek and lowly in heart: and ye shall find rest unto your souls" (Matthew 11:28).

There is a real "Christmas tree" for all of us. It isn't festooned with tinsel! It stands on a bare, ugly hill.

But on it God the Father in love gave this world His eternal Gift in the person of His Son Jesus, "that whosoever believeth in him, should not perish, but have everlasting life."

You will begin to be merry and rejoice the day you arise and go to the Father and say, "Father, I have sinned. . . . " The joy of the homecoming begins with the Father's kiss of forgiveness, and the heart that is merry because his sins are forgiven is only *beginning* to be merry. The joy continues until it flows like a river and blesses not only his life but the lives of all it touches.

10
He's Your Brother

The special welcome, the merry songs, the sounds of rejoicing occasioned by the homecoming of the Prodigal jangled in the ears of his elder brother, busy in the field. So, pouting, "he would not go in." He was not only disinterested, he was angry. He thought evangelism was a waste of time and money. So he made himself conspicuous by his absence. His main objections, sullenly articulated, have not changed much through succeeding generations.

THAT MUSIC!

To begin with, he did not like the music. "He heard music . . . and he called one of the servants and asked what these things meant" (Luke 15:25, 26).

It was happy, redemptive music. It got down into the feet of the crowd and made them feel like dancing. It had a sound of victory.

Everybody got caught up in the spirit of rejoicing—everybody, that is, except the elder brother. It offended him. He complained about it. Perhaps he thought it smacked of cheapness and lack of depth. He had no intention of endorsing such light music with his presence. "He . . . would not go in."

But concertos and long works of musical

mechanics prove cumbersome vehicles to express the
joy of men who have been brought back from the
pigpens of iniquity. They want to share their redemptive experiences in the language and the cadence of
the masses. They can find interpretation in "Love
Lifted Me" and "Hallelujah!" and "Let's Just Praise
the Lord."

SUCH EXPENSE!

Furthermore, the elder brother did not like to see
the expenditures his father was making on behalf of
this long-lost brother home from his wanderings.
"Thou hast killed for him the fatted calf" (Luke
15:30). His voice accuses his father. It is a popular
complaint from those who will "not go in." There is
too much time and effort spent in welcoming these
prodigals back, they contend. It is far better to con-
serve the assets for those who support the church. If
money is to be spent, it should be spent on them.

"Lo, these many years do I serve thee, neither transgressed I at any time thy commandment" (Luke
15:29). His was a record of goodness unsurpassed. He
was not one to object to an expenditure that would be
a bonus for his faithful service. More carpeting, a
more versatile organ, a better kitchen, easier seating,
central air conditioning would all be in order as long
as they were rewards for his faithful service.

But expenditures for evangelism were rightfully
questioned, from the elder brother's viewpoint. After
all, how long can you depend upon people who have
"wasted . . . substance with riotous living" (Luke
15:13)? It is a risky investment. And furthermore, they
are questionable company. Who wants to rub elbows
in the same pew with scoundrels who have transgressed and broken the commandments of God?

Today there is a tendency to expect tax money to take care of such problems. Let the government bureaus and antipoverty plans and urban renewal and assistance to depressed areas reach the stained and bankrupt. Turn the narcotic addict over to the federal clinic! Steer the drunkard toward a therapy group that meets privately for research into the kinds of problems he is facing. Send the young unmarried mother out of town to an agency that will arrange for the adoption of her child-to-be. Keep the "fatted calf" for the deserving member!

So he would have picketed the Sunday night service by his absence. He would not identify with the joyous attitude that says, "We are glad to see you here, sinner friend. The best we can offer you in Father's house is none too good."

In an attempt to placate the older son, the father of the Prodigal entreated him, "It was meet that we should make merry, and be glad: for this thy brother was dead, and is alive again, and was lost, and is found" (Luke 15:32).

But the older brother was one with those who think evangelists are a waste of time. In their expert opinion there is a far better way to spend the church's money, mainly on themselves. "He . . . would not go in."

Yet, from just a financial point of view, an evangelistic campaign that reaches even one family for Christ pays for itself through that family's tithes and offerings. But over and above that, how can you reckon its value in terms of the destiny of a human soul, changed by the grace of God?

"If he lose one of them, doth (he) not leave the ninety and nine in the wilderness, and go after that which is lost, until he find it? And when he hath found it, he layeth it on his shoulders, rejoicing. And

when he cometh home, he calleth together his friends
and neighbors, saying unto them, Rejoice with me; for
I have found my sheep which was lost" (Luke 15:4-6).

The Son of God put it this way in another story He
told: "But a certain Samaritan, as he journeyed, came
where he was: and when he saw him, he had compassion on him, and went to him, and bound up his
wounds, pouring in oil and wine, and set him on his
own beast, and brought him to an inn, and took care of
him; . . . and whatsoever thou spendest more, when I
come again, I will repay thee" (Luke 10:33-35).

WHAT ABOUT ME?

The elder brother did not like the father's attitude,
for another thing. In fact, that was the real rub. "Yet
thou never gavest me a kid, that I might make merry
with my friends" (Luke 15:29). He belonged to the
religious entertainment crowd. It is the crowd that
finds its fun in church suppers and picnics; in bowl-
ing and other games. These are the folk who claim the
church as their private corporation, "that I might
make merry with my friends." They substitute the
social for the spiritual and the evangelistic thrust.

God's answer to that complaint is, "All that I have is
thine." What have you appropriated from this Father
of mercy? What have you affirmed to be yours of His
grace and provision?

It was obvious the elder brother loved his father
even less than he did his brother. Today he would not
be so much concerned about the person in his church
who "prays through" as about "when will he be
through praying."

The radish in a backyard garden has more real religion than the person who takes such a self-centered
attitude. The radish affirms that the Creator will pro-

vide the color it needs. It reaches out for size and shape, for taste and distinctiveness. That radish accepts from the firmament rain and sunshine; nutrition and chemical. It takes at face value the fact that God says, "all that I have is thine."

It is a sin to act like a beggar and underprivileged person in the midst of such total supply as God makes available to us. Jacob drew a contract and became the Israel of God. Elijah drew fire and broke a national apostasy. Jonah drew repentance and turned an entire city around. Mary drew compassion, and out of her came seven devils. Peter drew a miracle, and Dorcas returned to life.

The possibilities are limitless. "Son, thou art ever with me, and all that I have is thine" (Luke 15:31).

Why do you go to church? You are there time and again, "ever with me." The community knows your profession. What have you accomplished with the grace of God? What will your answer be at Judgment? The means are at your disposal.

If anyone ever needed a friend, a sinner does. He has been stripped, abandoned, tormented, mocked, reduced to unspeakable poverty of spirit. It has been a long way back. Every step has been contested by the devil. Every thought has been an accusation, "I am no more worthy to be called a son." You cannot possibly comprehend what it means to have a robe instead of rags; a feast instead of famine; a kiss instead of a kick, if you haven't walked that road. How long has it been since you have considered any sinner your friend—a friend to be won, a brother to gain? "He . . . would not go in."

HE'S YOUR BROTHER

The older son did not like his brother. "Thy brother

91

is come" (Luke 15:27). That is what God says to us when the Prodigal comes home: "Thy *brother* is come."

Do you recognize him? He is a member of the human race. He is faced with the same alternative —hell or heaven. His soul can "be in want" or it can be clothed with righteousness. You are not looking at a customer or a digit or an item of population. You are looking at a brother.

He has been absent a long time. He has been deceived. He has been deserted. He remembers when he was so hungry that devils urged him to end it all. He has been so lonely that he would have been willing to crawl if it were possible to make it right again.

You should be the first to welcome him. Offer him a seat. Make him feel wanted. Place an arm around him when the invitation is given. Walk out and down the aisle toward the altar with him. Share your faith with him. "Thy brother is come."

What disturbs you? Is it the smell? God can and will change that. No one appreciates the odor of a pigpen. He has been there for some time. His very breath tells of wasted substance. He has blown out in smoke more assets than you have been able to put away in a bank. He has swallowed more "bubble water" with its illusions of grandeur than you have been able to afford in a similar expenditure for education. And yet his thirst has not been satisfied.

Yes, the fumes and the flames will die. "Bring forth the best robe, and put it on him; and put a ring on his hand, and shoes on his feet" (Luke 15:22). You will not know him to be the same person after God cleanses and clothes him. The angels are happy. God is happy. Why can you not be? "Thy brother is come."

What offends you? Is it his manners? Remember!

He has not been in polite company. It has been every man for himself where he came from. "And he began to be in want . . . and no man gave unto him" (Luke 15:14, 16). You stop being choosy when it can be said of you that you would "fain have filled (your) belly with the husks that swine did eat" (Luke 15:16). The gospel has a great sound to the man who has "spent all."

What about it? Are you still judging a man by the color of his skin, the year and vintage of his car, his grammar, the cut of his suit, his haircut, and his golf score? Will you be the next one to ask the question, "Who is my neighbor?" Do you really want an answer to that question? Look! "Thy brother is come." It is time now to "make merry, and be glad."

When you sin against your brother, you sin against your God. There is a crust of resentment that God in His mercy wants to break in your life. And when He does, the evangelistic service will have a rebirth in your community. And it will no longer be said, "He . . . would not come in." It will rather again be said, "You will have to go early to get a seat."

11
I'll Get Even

What a strange sullen note the elder brother sounds in the midst of the rejoicing of the family over the return of the Prodigal. It was a note of resentment —harsh, strident, unrelenting: "Thou never gavest me a kid, that I might make merry with my friends" (Luke 15:29).

Resentment is smoldering anger. These active volcanoes threaten us all today. Anger that has churned for generations, and has somehow been held in check, threatens to break loose and bury us in a lava flow of terrible retribution.

The nag and nudge in a man's soul to get even is based on the biggest lie in the universe. You never get even, never! Take a life, and you leave a home blighted by your act, a woman whose husband is locked away, children without a father, society without the benefit of that man's talents. No, that isn't an "equalizer" you hold in your hand! Murder is never the answer.

We all have "accounts receivable." There is not one of us who does not feel he has been shortchanged at some time in life. So we appoint ourselves the collectors just to get even—to balance things. But when we do, we always reach for a little more than is coming to us, for good measure, we say.

Only the gospel can act as an antibiotic to quench smoldering anger. If it does not, the little "gentleman" who endured the bullying with submissive smiles may commit psychopathic murder.

SUPPRESSED RAGE

This kind of murder happened in David's family. Absalom, a beautiful lad with sophisticated manners and gracious speech, "hated Amnon" for the humiliation he had caused Tamar, his sister, to bear. Then it happened: "Now Absalom had commanded his servants, saying, Mark ye now when Amnon's heart is merry with wine, and when I say unto you, Smite Amnon; then kill him, fear not" (2 Samuel 13:28).

It became a gory cocktail party. Rumor spread that Absalom had wiped out the entire royal family. But an advisor told David: "Amnon only is dead; for by the appointment of Absalom this hath been determined from the day that he forced his sister Tamar. . . . But Absalom fled" (2 Samuel 13:32, 34). Nothing was *evened*. It finally ended in a civil war.

Unless the gospel reaches something in the human heart, the moment can come when a person can go berserk with hostility. That repressed rage will reach a spilling-over point.

Perhaps the "elder brother" in this universal story of the Prodigal Son was an overindulged child, while the other boy may have been underindulged. It is possible. A child can be smothered by both attention and restriction. A child's life can be preempted. He may be reduced to an unvarying schedule by some parent, with no life of his own. He is not allowed to think for himself. He is not allowed to choose for

95

himself. He is denied individuality and the right and privacy to make mistakes. He exists as though he were in an incubator. Every wish is anticipated. He burns under the tyranny of a parent, who after the explosion, says, "I was only doing it for his own good."

A boy needs a spine as well as manners. He needs convictions even more than he needs the right kind of clothes. So he smolders! His secret dreams could terrify the adults around him. He steams with hatred.

Under the crust it is there. "Lo, these many years do I serve thee, neither transgressed I at any time thy commandment." ". . . And he was angry" (Luke 15:29, 28).

FRIGHTENING ANGER

This terrible anger is frightening. Races are seething. Cultures are resentful. The scales of justice tremble. There is no possible way of getting even. We have to find forgiveness. If we don't spill our need at the altars of God, we'll spill our resentment into the lives of those about us. Buried grudges are time bombs. Suppressed egos are miserable under social and intellectual confinement. Obedience is one thing, but too often it has been the wrong tag for obliteration.

What do these protests mean? They mean that once again there must be a great persuasion. It is one thing to win someone over. It is quite another thing to callously overrun someone. Only the gospel can search out and destroy this virus of resentment.

This steam and pressure must be converted into a drive for constructive action rather than for destructiveness. They present a priceless opportunity for new beginnings. "Son . . . all that I have is thine. It was meet that we should make merry, and be glad: for this thy brother was dead, and is alive again; and was lost, and is found" (Luke 15:31, 32). There can be an end to misunderstandings, to injustices, to grievances. New viewpoints are possible.

The greatest exhibition of forgiveness is in the death of Jesus Christ. The thief understood it. "But the other answering (his companion in crime) rebuked him, saying, Dost not thou fear God, seeing thou art in the same condemnation? And we indeed justly; for we receive the due reward of our deeds: but this man hath done nothing amiss. And he said unto Jesus, Lord, remember me when thou comest into thy kingdom" (Luke 23:40-42).

The Saviour turned all the railing, the mockery, the torment, the hideous miscarriage of justice, the unleashed sadism of professional people into a stream of pity, kindness, and redemption toward a crunched and twisted life.

Without that sublimation, resentment breaking loose turns riot into revolution, and cannot be stopped till it wears itself out. Read history again if you doubt it. Start with a study of the French Revolution. Various groups are going to be heard today. Make no mistake about it. Resentment has strength— the strength of a madman—the strength of insanity. Causes are going to be noticed today. They will not go away just because we are tired of seeing them on the front pages. They are persistent.

There are so many seeds for smoldering anger. Children resent parental restraint. Color is snubbed in the classroom. Brutality is suffered in the barracks. Favoritism is practiced in the office. Lies are fostered for profit. People feel stepped on. Brainwashed. Exploited. Slowly they reach the boiling point.

It could have made Joseph a militant. No one suffered more raw deals than the kid from Canaan. Then there came for him the moment that every discontented person on earth thirsts for—the moment to get even.

How did he handle it? His response to his brothers who had sold him as a slave is a guideline that has come down through generations: "Now therefore be not grieved, nor angry with yourselves, that ye sold me hither," he reassured his brothers. "For God did send me before you to preserve life. . . . So now it was not you that sent me hither, but God" (Genesis 45:5, 8).

I know it's hard to believe that such forgiveness exists. But only God can balance the scales of justice. "I will repay" is as much a guarantee as Calvary.

Bitterness can lie dormant for a long time. It did in Naomi. She didn't find it possible to turn away from three consecutive funerals in the family—those of her husband and her two sons—and not feel bitter. "Call me not Naomi, call me Mara: for the Almighty hath dealt very bitterly with me. I went out full, and the Lord hath brought me home again empty" (Ruth 1:20, 21).

She wanted to be isolated. She wanted to fester. She had more than the "blahs." She was resentful. She felt herself to be very much a part of a minority group.

The urge to get even is a terrible, malingering hell within. You feel persecuted and tormented inside. You feel worse than an untouchable. You feed on destruction. Something won't quit inside of you. It keeps eating away. The thirst for retaliation is stronger than a man's passion for drink. It intoxicates you. It urges you to be "Number One" if only for a moment—to see your name in the headlines, even though it is associated with tragedy. You go on hating. You go on lugging around a sense of guilt.

This passion for revenge is often the cause of physical distress. Competent medical doctors can tell you that. The remedy is reconciliation. Bring your bitterness to the altar. Hannah did. She was a woman provoked, needled, humiliated, disappointed. She came very near being a hateful, vengeful person instead of the mother of a man of God. "And she was in bitterness of soul, and prayed unto the Lord, and wept sore" (1 Samuel 1:10). And when she exposed her soul to the light of God's love, He healed her hurt and gave her the desire of her heart.

Job had to fight bitterness. "My soul is weary of my life; I will leave my complaint upon myself; I will speak in the bitterness of my soul" (Job 10:1). Bitterness did not make his tumors any easier to bear. It did not make his huge losses any less. He felt let down. For a little while his world had gone to pieces. He might have lost his mind. Yet, by God's grace he came to this saving conclusion, "Another dieth in bitterness of soul, and never eateth with pleasure" (Job 21:25). Comparing his lot with that of those who had never known the joys of a family or prosperity in any degree, he realized he had at least had more than many.

It's a long, long road that never has a turn in it. There are only three chapters in the Book of Ruth, but in those three chapters, Naomi's bitterness turns to unbounded happiness. Sometimes it takes a few more chapters.

There are 42 chapters in the Book of Job, but the story ends the same way. "So the Lord blessed the latter end of Job more than his beginning: for he had fourteen thousand sheep, and six thousand camels, and a thousand yoke of oxen. . . . He had also seven sons and three daughters" (Job 42:12, 13). That is some inventory for a man, who a few chapters back, had been on the ashpile!

ANTIDOTE FOR HATRED

The only medicine strong enough to banish hatred is forgiveness. Ernest Gordon reported the paranoiac hatred that enveloped the allied prisoners at Chungai for the cruelty and starvation to which they were subjected. He and his fellow prisoners were actually being consumed by the cancer of their resentment. They were not aware of their disease, but they were nonetheless its helpless victims. They fed on this disease of the soul. It had to be stopped or they would all perish.

Gordon identified that red-letter day when the necessary new spirit swept the prisoner-of-war camp. A young noncom was leading the men in the Lord's Prayer, only to find that his was the only voice repeating the words, "Forgive us our trespasses as we forgive those who trespass against us." He started the prayer again, and this time hundreds joined and began to sob. It was not only their salvation, but their recovery of health as well that was hanging on that one word "Forgive."

Malice will eat you to pieces. Antagonisms in your soul will destroy you. They will produce nihilism in a nation! It is a blind and unreasonable fury that wastes itself away in indiscriminate destruction. It leaves a shambles.

The apostle Paul remembered a time when his life was motivated by this smoldering anger, when he "made havoc of the church, entering into every house, and haling men and women, committed them to prison" (Acts 8:3).

But it all changed when he met Jesus. And he recalls what happened as he writes to Titus. "For we ourselves also were sometime foolish, disobedient, deceived, serving divers lusts and pleasures, living in malice and envy, hateful, and hating one another. But after that the kindness and love of God our Saviour toward men appeared" (Titus 3:3, 4).

That kindness and love of God saved a big man for history. The course of Paul's early hostility might have reduced him to anonymity. His madness could have destroyed him in his youth. Where then would be the immortal letters that bear his name? Where then would be the stately churches that call themselves "St. Paul's"? What mother would have named her son after the noble citizen of Tarsus?

Let me urge you to shun the destructive anger that threatens your very existence. Get rid of that time bomb lurking in your soul! Those slight tremors that awaken you in the night are a warning of convulsions to come. If there is a secret rage within you, you need a cleansing. You cannot get even. No man or group of men, can ever balance the accounts of history. God makes that His business. But you can find rest—in forgiving and being forgiven.

12
It's All Yours

The focus of this book has been largely on the Prodigal Son's adventures and return, including some of the universal and timeless truths growing out of this story. In this final chapter I am focusing on a profound, yet simple, truth. Jesus put it into the mouth of the father of the Prodigal as a means of soothing the frustrations of the elder brother: "Son, all that I have is thine" (Luke 15:31).

What would you think of a person who lived in poverty—with a fortune available to her of a quarter of a million dollars, and more than half of it in ready cash?

What would you think of that same person if you found her living in an old house, badly in need of paint and other repairs, with no electricity, and not even indoor plumbing? What would be your evaluation of this person, living amid squalor and filth, while fully aware that she had ample funds to live comfortably and normally?

You would probably agree with the county judge who stepped into the situation and declared this person incompetent to handle her own affairs. Probably born an heiress, this woman lived like a beggar. No one should live like that!

No one should live as though there was no God! It's more foolish to live as though there was no God than it is to live as though there was no modern heating or plumbing in this land where these things are the norm. "The fool hath said . . . there is no God." And only a fool would say in our society, "There is no electricity," or "There are no modern means of communication or education."

Only a fool lives as though God did not exist or was not accessible.

When someone says to me, "Brother Ward, I cannot afford to be a Christian," my answer is, "As for me, I cannot afford not to be a Christian." Let me put it in the words of the Bible, "The things which are impossible with men are possible with God." What a difference those two little words, "with God" can make in life. The man of the world who says to me, "You don't know what you're missing," doesn't know what *he's* missing. It is actually he who is living far below his privileges.

The Bible puts it this way, "Eye hath not seen, nor ear heard, neither have entered into the heart of man, the things which God hath prepared for them that love him."

THE ONLY STING

Have you ever stopped to ask yourself about what you are missing in life? The only sting to death is sin. Sin means "missing the mark—a mission unaccomplished." To catch one glimpse of eternity and to realize how foolishly and cheaply you have spent a lifetime while on earth, will bring a sting—a pain so sharp that it will make you want to cry out for another chance—one more chance to go through life, and this time include God in it!

When God says, "All that I have is thine," He backs up that statement with the record that He has sent His Son to die for our sins. Here is what the Bible says, "Let us therefore come boldly unto the throne of grace, that we may obtain mercy, and find grace to help in time of need."

And again it says, "If any of you lack wisdom, let him ask of God, that giveth to all men liberally, and upbraideth not, and it shall be given him."

There are over 5,000 promises in God's Word, promises like those I have just quoted. And the apostle James says, "ye have not because ye ask not." Ask yourself right now, "Am I living beneath my privilege? Am I a sinner, a rebel, burdened with a sense of trespass and unforgiveness when I could be a child of God and have my conscience void of offense? Am I facing divorce and the break-up of my home, the end of my dreams and efforts when I could count my years of married life a string of pearls, and gather my family around the open Book of God and hear my children open their hearts to God?"

Are you a tired worldling, tired of piling wealth upon wealth, tired of sophisticated forms of pleasure-seeking, tired of the empty vanity and chitchat of fellow worldlings? Have you starved your soul while overfeeding your body?

Have you done anything at all that men will thank God for when you have moved on? Have you grown bitter and cynical? Have you shut God out of your life and lived in a tight little world of your own choice?

Then let me tell you, you are missing it! You are living as though God was not available. You are carrying loads He wants to carry for you. You are wrestling with decisions He can guide you in making. You are depressed with regrets and sorrows He wants to wipe away. All that He has is ours! Take advantage of it.

THE REAL TROUBLE

The real trouble with many of us is that we are living far beneath our privileges. The elder brother in the story of the Prodigal Son complained to the father, "Lo, these many years do I serve thee, neither transgressed I at any time thy commandment, and yet thou never gavest me a kid that I might make merry with my friends. But as soon as this thy son was come, which hath devoured thy living . . . thou hast killed for him the fatted calf." That was the complaint.

And here is the answer to that complaint: "And he said unto him, Son, thou art ever with me, and all that I have is thine." The trouble with this "good man" was that he lived all the time as though no calf was available to him—as though no feast could be his—as though his friends would not be welcome—as though his father was a miser! The lack of appropriating faith was his real trouble. And perhaps it is your trouble, too. Are you living in Father's house, faithfully serving, yet quietly complaining of the fare?

What a different world it would be if all of us claimed everything our Heavenly Father has and wants to share with us as His own children.

Some years ago a district superintendent called upon a young couple who were ministering in a small church. He said to the young woman, "How are you getting along?"

"We manage to get along," she said, "though we do not have any surplus as a rule. But we always have something. God sees us through."

She went on to relate this experience: "On a certain Monday we were reduced to a single dollar, and my husband needed that to buy gasoline. But that evening we had been invited to attend a meeting in another church. We felt we wanted to give an offering if we attended, so we purposed to give the dollar.

"During the meeting someone gave me $10. The next morning I gave a dollar to my husband for the gasoline. During the morning I went to the coal dealer's and ordered a ton of the cheapest coal, for $9. The dealer said it was as easy to deliver two tons as one, but I explained that the $9 was all I had. He said he would deliver two tons and I could pay for the second whenever I had the money.

"That afternoon a lady came to visit me, and as she was leaving she gave me $10. I went to the coal dealer and paid for the second ton. Thus, everything we needed was supplied and we still had $1 left."

This couple was far from rich, but they had learned the secret of drawing upon the divine supply. For them, "All that I have is thine" was more than a text in the Bible. It was a divine assurance that God would supply their need for ordinary things like coal and gasoline and food, and He did not disappoint them.

Let me call your attention to these words from the Bible: "Beloved, now are we the sons of God," and "All things are yours." "Ask, and it shall be given you; seek, and ye shall find; knock, and it shall be opened unto you: for everyone that asketh receiveth; and he that seeketh findeth; and to him that knocketh it shall be opened."

VIEWPOINT

On the outside looking in, the Prodigal knew that even the hired servants had "bread enough and to spare." Living at home in the midst of plenty, never having known hunger, or thirst, or cold, or humiliation, or loneliness, the elder brother had to be reminded, "Son, all that I have is thine."

Wherever these words find you in relation to Father's house—outside looking in, or inside enjoying His blessings—may you appropriate by God's grace all that He has for you. "For everyone that asketh receiveth; and he that seeketh findeth; and to him that knocketh it shall be opened."